20th Hussars
in the Great War

BY

MAJOR J. C. DARLING, D.S.O.

PUBLISHED PRIVATELY BY THE AUTHOR, HOMELAND,
LYNDHURST, HAMPSHIRE . . . MCMXXIII

DEDICATION.

To those gallant fellows who gave their lives in the service of their King and Country and in upholding the good name of the 20th Hussars this book is most humbly dedicated.

PREFACE.

The 20th Hussars do not pretend that they won the war. As Colonel Richardson said, at the first Regimental dinner after the armistice, "all we claim is that whenever we were given a job to do, we did it". In this little book I have tried to describe the jobs we were given and how we did them. If my descriptions are inaccurate I beg to be excused, my defence being that it was not until after the Regiment had been disbanded that it was suggested that I should write the book. I have not been able to consult many of those who would have given me great assistance. Those I have consulted have taken a lot of trouble to give me all the information they could, and to them are due my best thanks.

CONTENTS.

Chapter		Page
I.	WE GO TO WAR	1
II.	MONS AND THE RETREAT	8
III.	THE MARNE AND AISNE	33
IV.	THE FIRST BATTLE OF YPRES	41
V.	1915 AND 1916	56
VI.	1917, ARRAS AND LEMPIRE	73
VII.	BATTLE OF CAMBRAI, NOVEMBER 1917,	85
VIII.	SPRING AND SUMMER, 1918, (THE GERMAN OFFENSIVE)	93
IX.	AUGUST 1918, BATTLE OF AMIENS	106
X.	THE LAST PUSH	117

LIST OF ILLUSTRATIONS.

LIEUT.-COLONEL G. T. C. EDWARDS, C.B.	facing Page	1
MAP ONE	,,	5
MAP TWO	,,	41
MAP THREE	,,	57
LIEUT.-COLONEL G. T. R. COOK, D.S.O.	,,	73
LIEUT.-COLONEL A. C. LITTLE, D.S.O.	,,	106

INTRODUCTION

BY

LIEUT.-GENERAL SIR PHILIP CHETWODE, BART.,
K.C.B., K.C.M.G., D.S.O.

My dear Darling,

I am very glad you have taken the trouble to place on record the more intimate doings of your distinguished regiment, the 20th Hussars, in the Great War. I congratulate you on the result which I have read with the greatest interest.

No regiment of cavalry entered upon the great adventure better trained and prepared for war than the 20th, and the value of that good training in peace time was apparent from the first day they met the enemy. All ranks were imbued with a splendid spirit and knew exactly what to do in the many arduous and difficult tasks they had to perform.

I was proud to have under my command the regiment on which I could always depend no matter what I asked them to do. The 5th Brigade were, as you say, a happy family not only because they got on well together, but because the various units knew they could always depend on each other absolutely.

It is tragic to think that the regiment with such a fine record has, for the moment, lost its full status as a separate regiment. No one will rejoice more than I shall when they regain it.

Yours ever,

PHILIP W. CHETWODE.

COMMAND HEADQUARTERS,
ALDERSHOT.
4th July, 1923.

Lieut.-Colonel G. T. G. Edwards, C.B.

CHAPTER I.—We go to War.

(See Map I.)

WHEN war first threatened and then broke out in Europe in 1914, the 20th Hussars, commanded by Lieut.- Col. G. T. G. Edwards, were stationed at Colchester, where they had been since 1911. They formed a unit of the 5th Cavalry Brigade under Brig.-Gen. Sir Philip Chetwode. The other regiments of the Brigade were the Royal Scots Greys and the 12th Royal Lancers, stationed respectively at York and at Norwich. These regiments were no strangers to the 20th. We had been brigaded with the Greys at Pond Farm, on Salisbury Plain, during the manœuvres of 1908; and while we were there together the regiments had got to know one another very well. Since the 12th had come to Norwich we had seen a good deal of them; and the officers, at any rate, had become acquainted with one another. We thus found ourselves destined to fight alongside two regiments whose fine soldierly qualities we had already appreciated in peace. As time went on the good feeling and mutual confidence existing between the three regiments became more and more marked, and I think I can say without fear of being contradicted that throughout the British Army no happier family existed during the War than the 5th Cavalry Brigade.

I do not intend to dwell long on the events following the receipt of the order to mobilize. This was received about 6.15 p.m. on the 4th of August. Everything proceeded " according to plan " with a clockwork-like monotony that did the highest credit to those who had been responsible for the mobilization scheme. Reservists arrived in batches from the Depôt at Scarborough, and officers on detached duties hastened to rejoin. Major Richardson had just finished his time as Adjutant of the South Devon Yeomanry, and in his haste to be in time for the

Chapter I.

hunt he drove his Ford car from Exeter to Colchester throughout the night, and reached barracks about breakfast time.

I need hardly recall the zeal with which Officers of the Reserve volunteered to join their old Corps, or the keenness among men of all ranks, reservists as well as serving soldiers, to be included among the original Expeditionary Force. Similar scenes must have occurred in every barracks. The C.O. had indeed a hard job in settling who was to go. Many had to stay behind and bide their time.

The only officer from the Reserve who accompanied the regiment to France was Captain S. H. Cristy, D.S.O.

Horses arrived almost daily, the stables in barracks were soon filled, and a remount camp was started at Middlewick. Thus, by the appointed day, the regiment was up to strength in officers, men and horses.

I think I am right in saying that it was during the afternoon of Saturday, 15th August, that the news leaked out in the mess and in the barrack rooms that the regiment was to leave Colchester the following day. The secret had been well kept.

Before going any further, it may be of interest to give the names of the officers, warrant officers and some of the senior N.C.O.'s who accompanied the regiment. I therefore set them out in the following table :—

Officer Commanding Regiment, Lieut.-Col. G. T. G. Edwards.
Second in Command, Major G. T. R. Cook.
Adjutant, Capt. G. A. Sanford.
Signalling Officer, Capt. J. C. Darling.
Machine Gun Officer, Lieut. J. K. McConnel.
Quartermaster, Lieut. W. Adams.
Regimental Sergt.-Major, Mr. Austin.
Regimental Quartermaster-Sergt., R.Q.M.S. Addis.
Farrier-Major, F.Q.M.S. Churchill.

Squadrons.	"A" Squadron.	"B" Squadron.	"C" Squadron.
O.C. Squadron	Major M. E. Richardson	Capt. A. C. Little	Capt. C. G. Mangles
2nd in Command	Lieut. W. H. M. Micholls	Capt. S. H. Cristy, D.S.O.	Capt. S. Barne.
O.C. 1st Troop	Lieut. G. W. I. Bairstow	Lieut. D. S. Peploe	Lieut. R. W. Sparrow
O.C. 2nd Troop	Lieut. J. T. Upton	Lieut. H. M. Soames	Lieut. D. C. M. Beech.
O.C. 3rd Troop	Lieut. J. Galbraith	Lieut. W. D. A. Hall	Lieut. R. M. Thompson

1914

O.C. 4th Troop	Lieut. W. A. Silvertop	Lieut. S. Carew	Lieut. J. H. Goodhart
S.S.M. ...	...S.S.M. Morwood	S.S.M. Wyborn	S.S.M. Smith
S.Q.M.S.	...S.Q.M.S. Stratford	S.Q.M.S. Traylen	S.Q.M.S. Whittingham

All details not accompanying the regiment joined the 13th Reserve Cavalry Regiment, which took over the barracks at Colchester, under the command of Lieut.-Col. A. M. B. Jones late 20th Hussars. This regiment was formed to supply drafts to make good casualties in the 14th and 20th.

The "first reinforcement," which was proceeding overseas almost simultaneously with the regiment, was under the command of Lieut. Dodgson. Sergt.-Major Clemenson, of orderly room fame, was destined to watch over our interests from the advanced base.

The following seconded officers did not accompany the regiment :—

Major Jennings-Bramly (serving with the Egyptian Army).
Major J. S. Cawley (Brigade-Major, 1st Cavalry Brigade).
Capt. E. W. P. Love (Adjutant, Duke of Lancaster's Own Yeomanry).
Capt. F. B. Hurndall (Adjutant, Berkshire Yeomanry).
Capt. R. H. Osborne (Instructor at the Cavalry School became on Mobilization, Staff Captain, 1st Cavalry Brigade).

It was about 7 a.m. on Sunday, 16th August, 1914, that the regiment began to entrain at St. Botolph's Station, Colchester, for "an unknown destination." Far more unknown was what the future might hold in store for us. I do not think many of us were worrying much about what was ahead of them. We had our best pals with us. We were off on this, the greatest adventure of our lives. We formed part of a regiment which each one considered was second to no other, and which we felt sure would do its duty, come what might. If any, more inquisitive than the rest, tried to discern the future, I am quite sure not one came anywhere near the truth in guessing the course of the momentous events which were crowded into the next few weeks—events in which each one was destined to act his little part.

Some may have guessed that within six days we should be in touch with the Germans; but I do not think any anticipated that within eight days the British Army would be in full retreat.

As our train, having skirted the northern suburbs of

Chapter I.

London, emerged on to the main line of the South Western Railway, it became obvious that we were bound for Southampton. The various trains reached Southampton Docks during the afternoon and evening. "A" Squadron embarked that night; the rest of us went to a rest camp, as our ship, the "Indore," was not ready. Our reception at Southampton was a most cordial one, though the town had by now become accustomed to troops passing through on the way to France. The following day, Monday, 17th, Regimental Headquarters "B" and "C" Squadrons embarked, and at 4 a.m. on the 18th sailed for the "unknown port." We reached Le Havre about 6 p.m.

The scene was one not quickly to be forgotten. As the transport approached, cheers broke out from the crowds collected on the pier. The cheers were answered from the ship. Some of the bolder spirits even experimented with their French by shouting "Vive la France" in answer to the "Vive l'Angleterre" of our gallant allies. Already small French boys had learnt to shout for "biscuits," of which the men seemed to have plenty to spare. I do not remember that as yet there were any cries for " du bully beef."

The work of disembarking proceeded slowly, yet surely. The only untoward incidents were when Lieut. Goodhart and two horses fell down two decks into the hold, and when Sergt.-Major Lee's horse was dropped by the crane on to the quay and got loose. Whether that gallant steed intended returning to his native shores or not, it is vain to conjecture. Certain it is that he leapt into the sea and swam out into the harbour. After a cruise round, however, he seems to have settled that desertion when on active service would bring discredit on his regiment. He therefore returned to the ship and got wedged in between it and the quay. From that position he was rescued at no small personal risk by Lieut. McConnel, who contrived to get down and fasten a rope round him, thus early demonstrating his readiness to take on any job that was going. This incident took place by the scanty light of a few gas jets on the wharf. The unloading went on all night, and was not finished till early the next morning. The regiment, as it landed, spent the night 18th—19th in one of the goods yards on the quay. On the morning of the 19th we set out, guided by a diminutive boy scout, to find "La Gare." We found it and entrained.

The progress of the train was leisurely, as is the way of troop trains in France. The men, seated in the open trucks that are labelled "Hommes 40, Chevaux 8," had ample opportunity to exchange salutations with the population, consisting mostly of women, who turned out to see the train go by. Girls threw bunches of flowers into the cattle trucks, often shouting for "Souvenirs" in return.

I am afraid not a few cap badges were deficient by the end of the journey.

The reception given to the British Army was magnificent. Everyone realised that this "Entente Cordiale" of which they had heard so much was a very live reality. When the train halted, the engine-driver was only too pleased to supply hot water from the boiler for making tea. The station masters and other officials were very important and busy. One station master in particular was most scrupulous in demanding from the Colonel to know whether the contents of the train were quite accurately represented on the document in his possession. With pride he showed us his 1870 medal. He had been through it in "Soixante-dix," and now had come the time for "la revanche." Everyone was in the best of spirits. The enthusiasm of the French nation had infected us.

At midday we stopped at Rouen, where the men got a meal and horses were watered and fed. Then the train lumbered on again. Towards evening the journey began to become tedious. Night came on and found us still rumbling through the monotonous French landscape. We slept as best we could, and woke next morning to find ourselves arriving at Hautmont. Here at last we were released. Our train journey was at an end. We were greeted by our Staff Captain, Capt. Willie Palmer, an old 20th himself, though now a 10th Hussar. He gave us the programme with his usual assurance—for all the world as if he had arranged it himself. "To-day we rest; to-morrow we march; and Monday *la grande bataille*." Hautmont is not far from Maubeuge, and after detraining we marched to Limont-Fontaine, a few miles away, where we went into billets. We were joined here by Lieut. Harlet of the French Artillery. He was our liaison officer,

Chapter I.

and brought with him twelve French N.C.O.'s as interpreters. One was sent to each troop.

We left Limont early on the morning of Friday, 21st, for the Brigade rendezvous, which was on the Maubeuge-Avesnes road. From there the Brigade, consisting of Greys, 12th, 20th, " J " Battery R.H.A., and 5th Cavalry Field Ambulance, marched, skirting Maubeuge, via Jeumont and Euquelines. Between these last two places we crossed the frontier into Belgium. The population all turned out and gave us a tremendous reception, being profuse with their offers of flowers, cigars and wine. As we were moving at a trot there was not much opportunity for accepting these tokens of hospitality. The march continued by Merbes-le-Chateau and Merbes-Ste.-Marie. At the latter place there were rumours of Germans somewhere. Rifles were loaded. Lieut. Beech and Lieut. Sparrow were sent off in command of patrols, but found nothing. Lieut. Beech was also to try and get touch with French cavalry on our right. It will be as well here to note the rôle of our brigade at this phase.

The British Army, as is well known, was disposed at the battle of Mons on the left flank of the Allies; 1st Corps on the right, 2nd on the left, Cavalry Division, under General Allenby, patrolling to the front and guarding the left flank. General Allenby's Division consisted of the 1st, 2nd, 3rd and 4th Cavalry Brigades. The 5th Cavalry Brigade was not under his command. It had originally been told off as " protective " cavalry, whereas the Division was " independent." Actually we were disposed on the extreme right of the British Army, and our rôle at this time was to reconnoitre to the front and to keep touch between the right of the 1st Corps and the left of the French 5th Army, under General De Lanrezac who were holding a line running roughly east and west through Charleroi. The French cavalry we were looking for was a cavalry corps who had already done considerable fighting in Belgium, and who had fallen back to cover the left of the 5th Army.

I think I am right in saying that the Merbes-Ste. Marie to Binche road, up which our brigade advanced, was the dividing line between the French and British Armies. We halted for the night just short of Binche. " B " Squadron were disposed :—Two troops under Capt. Little at Buvrinnes,

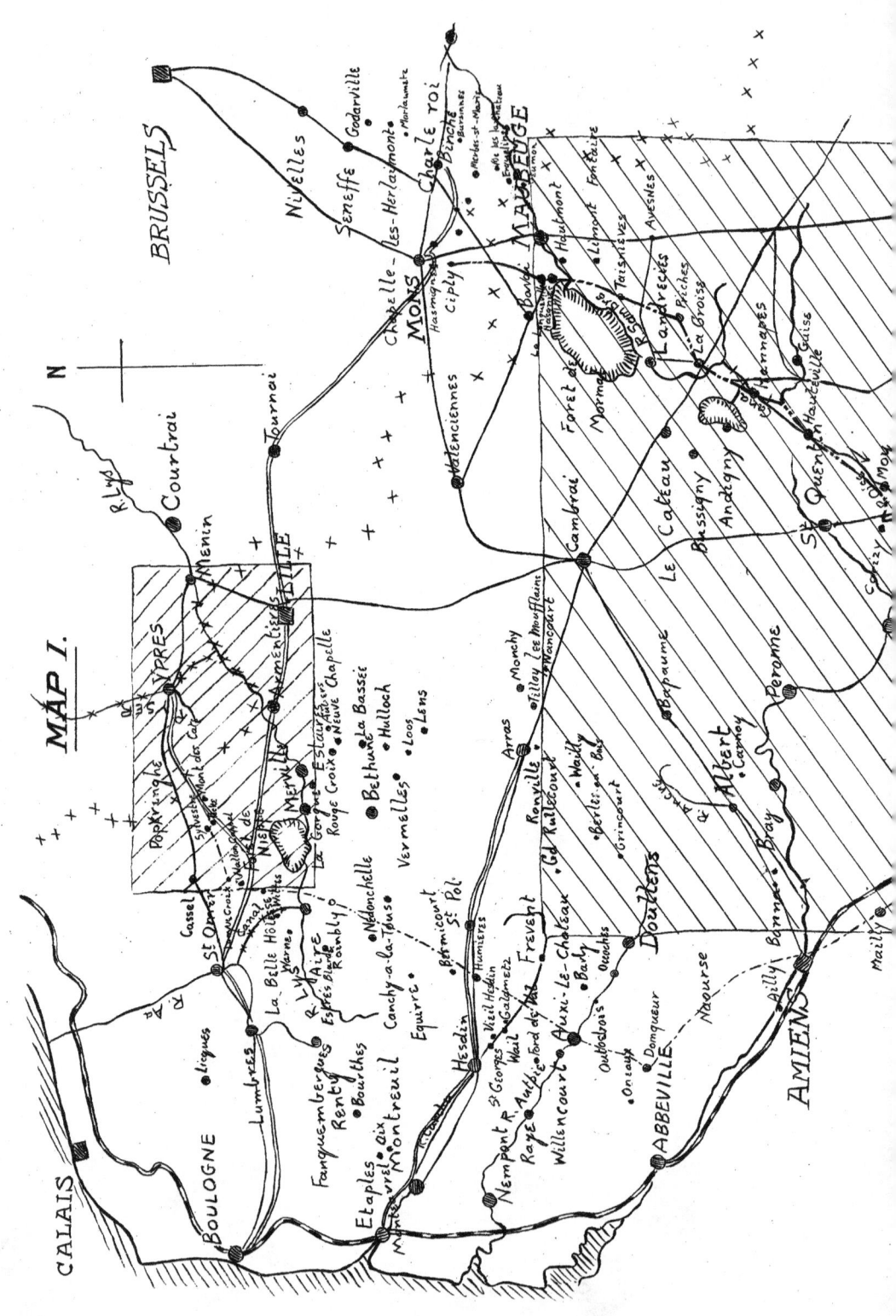

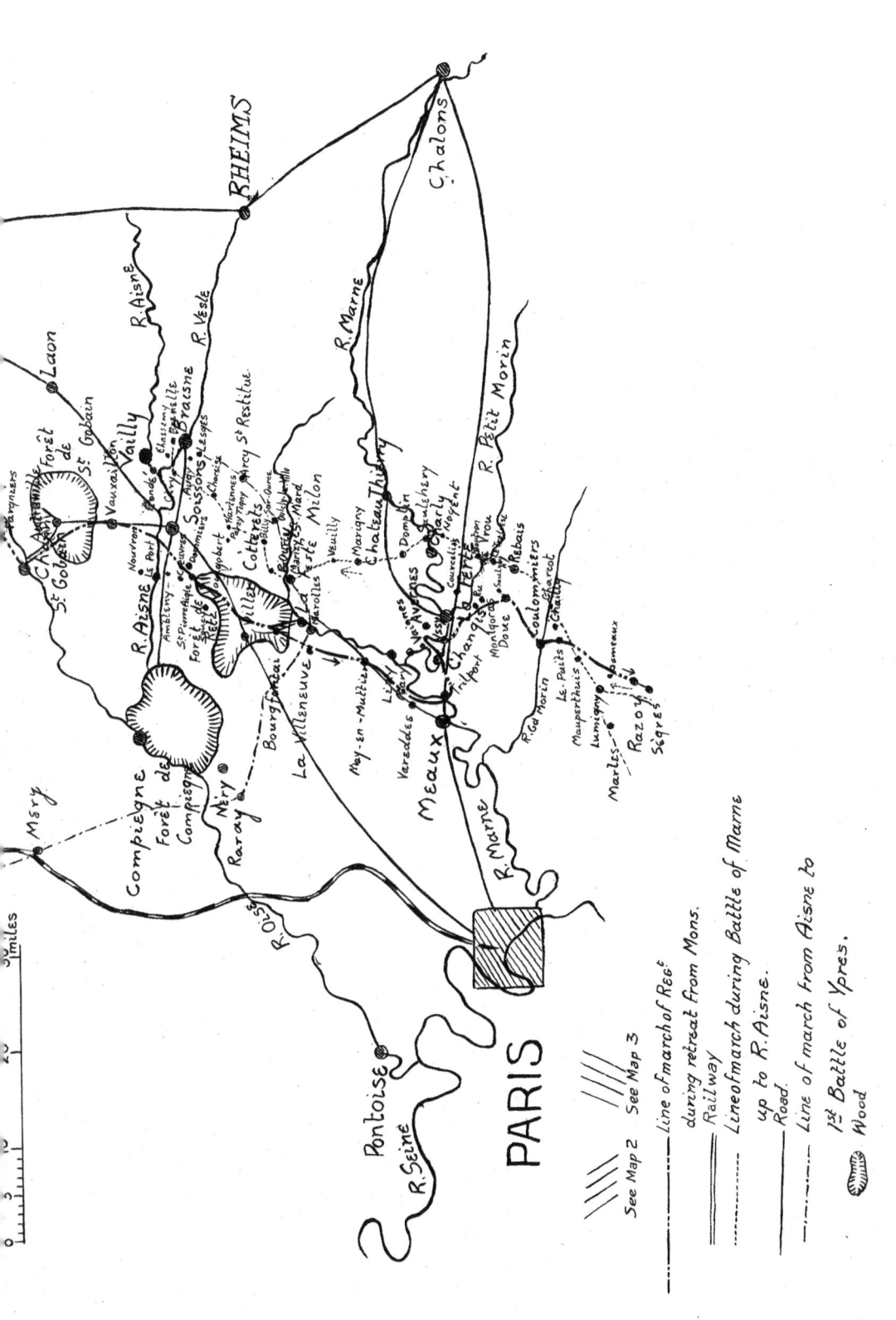

two troops under Capt. Cristy at Binche Station. "A" and "C" Squadrons bivouacked about one mile south of Binche, each squadron being responsible for its own protection. Lieut. Sparrow had taken a patrol to Morlanmetz, north-east of Binche, but met no enemy. The only attack during the night was made on "C" Squadron; it was repulsed by Capt. Mangles and Lieut. Beech. The attacking force turned out to be a cow! Lieut. Goodhart and Lieut. Harlet went on a liaison patrol in the evening, and got in touch with the French 10th Hussars.

That same evening the Brigadier ordered two officers' patrols, each of ten men, to be ready to march at 4 a.m. The officers (Lieuts. Thompson and Goodhart) went to Brigade Headquarters and got their orders that night. Lieut. Thompson was to go to Chapelle-les-Herlaimont and on to Godarville, if no enemy were encountered sooner. Lieut. Goodhart was to go to Seneffe.

During the night some French cavalry passed through Binche. Capt. Cristy, who knew French well, made a copy of a report of theirs on the situation of the 5th French Army and sent it to Brigade Headquarters. I fancy that this report made it clear that the French about Charleroi were pretty hard pressed.

So now we were really at war, and looking for Germans. I will take a new chapter to describe our first encounter with them.

CHAPTER II.—Mons and the Retreat.

(See Map I.)

IN recounting the experiences of Lieut. Thompson's patrol, I quote word for word his own account as it appears in his diary, which he has very kindly placed at my disposal. He writes :—

"*22nd August.* At 4 a.m. Goodhart and I went out on our first patrol. Breakfast, 3.15 a.m., with the aid of candles. It was most exciting going through Binche in the early morning, and one could hardly realise it was real war. Goodhart left me after going about two miles, and branched off to the left. Nothing much happened till I got to Chapelle-les-Herlaimont, about seven miles from Binche, except that we saw empty cartridge cases, etc., which showed the French had been having a fight there the day before. At Chapelle there were barricades, and a civilian came in very excited on a bike and said he had been fired on. I was also told by the burgomaster that a German officer had been there in the early morning and had said that the inhabitants would be treated all right provided there was no resistance. As there were no Germans at Chapelle, I went on towards Godarville, about 25 miles from Brussels. On my way I came in with a patrol of French Hussars, three men and a corporal, who said they had encountered a German patrol and killed one German. I saw no signs of any Germans at Godarville, so we went after the German patrol, and as my advanced point was entering Chapelle on the return journey he saw a German column moving along the road, transport he said, so we were evidently well behind them; I then had to get back somehow, so we made a dash to some woods which were about a mile off. On the way we were fired at by dismounted cavalry at long range. O'Shaughnessy's horse fell, and we had to leave him, as we were going at the gallop. We eventually got through the woods back to Binche, after turning and twisting all over the place. At one place I was shown a brigade of German cavalry in mass, halted; from here the station master telephoned to the next station to know if the Germans were there or not. As they were not, we made a bolt for it along the line, passing within 400 yards of a German patrol who took no notice of us, evidently thinking we were Germans. I was never more pleased to see Hall's face in my life than I was when we reached Binche Station, which he had been barricading. Got commended by the General on my patrol. When we reached Regimental Headquarters near Binche, the interpreter who was with me fell off his horse, saying ' It is too much,' into a faint. He had not ridden for sixteen years, and we had done about thirty miles in pretty quick time." Most of the interpreters were in the same state as the one described above, being reservists. They must have found their saddles very hard after a bit. Pte. O'Shaughnessy rejoined the regiment about five days later, having put on civilian clothes, and acted deaf and dumb when spoken to.

Lieut. Goodhart's objective, Seneffe, is about ten miles north of Binche on the road to Nivelles. For two or three miles out of Binche he found the country quite open. Crops had been carried, and there was nothing but stubble on the fields. After this the country was enclosed. I will now quote his own account of his experiences :—

"On the way I saw three or four hostile patrols (each 25-30 strong) on each of my flanks, but none were within a mile of my route. On arrival at Seneffe, inhabitants reported that some German cavalry were at the level crossing and station, which was at the bottom of a fairly steep hill which formed the main street. At the top of this hill I halted, and saw below me at the station, which was 800 yards away, 50 cavalrymen dismounted. A hostile patrol was just starting out up the hill, so I dismounted and gave strict orders that no one was to fire until I gave the order. The excitement was, however, too much for the trained " scout " of my troop. He blazed off at the two points at about 300 yards, and missed. I then withdrew my patrol. When I got clear of the enclosed country I halted. A civilian on a bicycle coming from the direction of

Chapter II.

the enemy overtook me. He seemed most friendly, and told me he lived close by, and that Lieut. the Earl of Leven and Melville and a troop of Scots Greys had spent the previous night at his farm, and that he had passed this troop a short time before retiring towards Binche. Very soon afterwards I saw on the road he had mentioned a strong troop, about 25 men, mounted on dirty-coloured horses (resembling greys dyed with Condy's). They were about a mile away. My signaller tried to semaphore to them with two service caps, but I was not surprised when they took no notice. (Why did he not use a flag?—Signalling Officer.) I therefore left my patrol, and rode over by myself to 'liaise' with them. I got quite close to them before I realised that they were carrying lances and were Huns. I returned to my patrol at a gallop. Part of the way lay along a pavé road running through a deep cutting. I looked round and saw an ugly Hun with a lance not more than two horses' lengths behind me. After that I gave my whole attention to keeping my horse on his legs on the pavé." Lieut. Goodhart does not relate that he tried to shoot the Hun with his revolver, and only then discovered that he had forgotten to load it. Anyway, the polo pony he was riding (well-known in the regiment, but not by a very complimentary name) seems to have beaten the Boche for pace, and to have enabled him to rejoin his patrol. He then withdrew through the outposts at Binche, and reported to the Brigadier. In this little brush with the enemy, the patrol captured three Hun horses. These created quite a stir on being brought in to the regiment, as being the first booty captured from the Germans. The Bosche saddles and accoutrements were great objects of interest, the horses did not compare favourably with our own.

It will be noticed that the Germans employed much stronger cavalry patrols than we did. They seemed, however, to be lacking in enterprise, and I doubt if they collected as valuable information as did our "eyes and ears of the Army."

The 1st troop "C" Squadron (Lieut. Sparrow) moved out north of Binche to support these patrols and assist their retirement if necessary. This troop encountered some German cavalry a bit north of Binche, and planned a little attack in conjunction with a strong patrol of French cavalry. It was agreed that our troop should use fire action while the French charged. It will be remembered that French cavalry, at this time, possessed nothing but carbines in the way of firearms. These were of very little use. The scheme miscarried, as the enemy could not be tempted to come very close, and the charge was delivered prematurely. The Germans retired at full gallop on to their squadron, and the French cavalry eventually had to withdraw. About the same time Lieut. Goodhart's patrol came by, the retirement of both these bodies being covered by the First Troop of " C " Squadron who then, in their turn, withdrew.

I have given the doings of these patrols in some detail as being the first encounters with the enemy which the regiment experienced in the Great War. From these it is seen that men of the regiment were in action against the Germans by about 8 a.m. on Saturday, 22nd August. We must thus have been one of the first units of the British Army to become engaged. During the morning of this day we remained in position guarding the southern outskirts of Binche. " B " Squadron got in touch with the 10th French Hussars on our right, in fact we were the extreme right flank unit of the B.E.F. On our left were the Greys, who were attacked by some Germans during the morning. No enemy approached our own position. The 12th Lancers remained in Brigade reserve. During the evening the regiment was withdrawn to Fauroeulx, about five or six miles south-west of Binche. Here we spent the night. Lieut. Bairstow took a patrol as far as Binche early the next morning.

On Sunday, 23rd August, the brigade moved soon after dawn to the Binche-Bavai road. Here the regiment, who were in brigade reserve, spent most of the day. Horses were off saddled. "A" Squadron found local protection. About noon, " B " Squadron were sent to reconnoitre to the right front. A patrol under Lieut. Soames encountered some Germans, and that officer was killed, one man was wounded, and two were missing. Lieut. Soames had been one of the cheeriest fellows in the regiment, and his death was a great blow. In him we lost one who, I am certain, would have proved a first-rate leader.

About 5 p.m. we moved to a sugar factory south-west of Givry. On our way there we had our first view of German shrapnel bursting. It was, however, a long way short of us.

Chapter II.

Indeed, it may not have been intended for us at all. The brigade moved across country, but encountered several obstacles that caused delay by making us form on a narrow front. It quite reminded us of manœuvres at home, but I think we took rather a delight in not having to dodge crops. Even fields of beet were taken in line by troop columns just as they came. We discovered that they do not make ideal ground to drill over. From the high ground near the sugar factory, a good view could be obtained of the battle that was going on north of Givry. Our infantry and artillery could be plainly seen in action.

A party from Regimental Headquarters was sent to Givry to reconnoitre the crossing over the stream and to cut the wire fences on the way, in case the brigade wished to cross either to support the infantry, or to deliver a counter-attack. We were not, however, called upon to act, and soon after dusk the order came for the whole brigade to settle down near the sugar factory for the night.

The R.E. had rigged up some water troughs, but the roads were very much congested; very few officers had seen the place in daylight, and there was considerable delay and a little confusion before all the horses got watered. In the end this was accomplished, and squadrons got settled in a stubble field, the only people under cover, if I remember right, being the officers of Regimental Headquarters, who shared the sugar factory with some of the Greys. Here we discovered some oats—a welcome find, as forage had not yet arrived. Considering we were competing in a friendly way with the canny Scotsmen, I think it was to our credit that our horses got quite a fair share of the swag. Rations arrived soon after midnight.

On Monday, 24th, we saddled up at 4 a.m., and moved off to the main Mons-Maubeuge road. Here we took up a position to cover the retirement of the 2nd Infantry Division. The regiment was disposed as follows:—On the left " B " Squadron at Ciply, on the right " A " Squadron, about half a mile east of the main road, on the Mons-Harmignies-Binche Railway. Machine Gun Section on the right in rear of " A " Squadron. " C " Squadron (support squadron) and R.H.Q. on the main road about one mile south of the railway.

By the time the regiment was in position, the retirement of the infantry had been going on for some time. We had not been there very long before the infantry rear guard passed through us. The main road, and ground held by the regiment, was all pretty heavily shelled with shrapnel by the Germans; but fortunately we sustained very few casualties. What there were were chiefly in "A" Squadron. About noon, the order came to retire. "A" Squadron were withdrawn first to a sunken lane on some high ground about one mile in rear of the original position, "C" taking up a position further back. Just before "B" got the order to retire, some German infantry or dismounted cavalry debouched in close order from a wood north of Ciply. "B" Squadron opened rapid fire on them at long range. This seems to have taken them by surprise and, we hope, inflicted some casualties. Anyway, the enemy's advance stopped dead. Captain Little was able to withdraw his squadron in rear of "A" without being in any way molested or even followed up. The whole regiment then withdrew about four miles to a position that had already been selected by the Brigadier and reconnoitred by Major Cook. We reached this position about 4 p.m., and held it till 7 p.m., when a further retirement was ordered.

Our patrols had been in touch with German cavalry patrols, but the latter were unenterprising, and probably unsupported, and never got near our main position. Soon after 7 p.m. we started for La Longueville, which was to be our billeting area for the night. After passing through the infantry rearguard our progress was very slow, as the roads were congested by troops and vehicles of every description. We marched through La Longueville to Hargnies, which was reached about 11 p.m. From our first position near Ciply, this was a retirement of twelve miles as the crow flies. This action was really typical of a successful cavalry rearguard. We had relieved the infantry of their responsibilities and anxieties throughout a long summer's day, holding successive positions while they had time to put many miles between themselves and the pursuing enemy. The one time the Germans threatened an attack we had checked them by a burst of rifle fire at long range. Finally, we had used our mobility to break off the engagement and make a long retirement, eventually getting

Chapter II.

behind our own infantry again for the night.

The morning of the 25th we were on the move about 4.30 a.m. The brigade got into position north of Hargnies to cover the retirement of the infantry. The regiment was in brigade reserve, where it remained all day. Some of " C " Squadron were employed patrolling into the Foret de Mormal, which was on our left flank, but none of them became engaged with the enemy. About 6 p.m., orders were received to retire to Taisnieres for the night. This was a distance of about eight miles as the crow flies. We crossed the Sambre, and noticed that the line of the river had been prepared for defence. It was obvious, however, that there was now no intention of holding it.

Soon after this we overtook a column of French transport waggons. They were a curious collection, consisting chiefly of civilian carts of every description, drawn by a varied assortment of horses. I am not wishing in any way to cast aspersions on our gallant Allies when I say that the appearance of this column was rather a shock to us. Their march discipline was bad. They brought back vividly to mind the pictures and accounts in history of the retreat of some beaten army. Our own army was retiring, but we knew that it was an orderly retirement, brought about by orders coming from higher authority, and that it had not been forced upon us by any tactical defeat. The men we were passing on the road had, however, the appearance of having " been through it." It was obvious that the force they belonged to had sustained a reverse, to put it mildly. The truth got home to us that somewhere away to our right flank all was not well with the Allied Army.

Our progress, mixed up as we now were with the French column on the same road, was necessarily very slow, and it was dark long before we were near our billets. All this time heavy artillery fire could be heard away to the north-east. In our immediate rear all was silent. Suddenly, out of the darkness a few rifle shots rang out on our left, as we were marching south, or rather as we were facing south during one of the many halts caused by the congestion of the road.

The bullets passed uncomfortably close over our heads, but it was at first thought that they must come from French or

British troops who had mistaken us for the enemy. Major Richardson, with some men of " A " Squadron and an interpreter named Gibert, who was a very good fellow, went in the direction of the firing and tried the effect of the French password. They were greeted with a volley, no doubt from a German patrol. Just then the column moved on again, and no more was seen or heard of the enemy. I mention this incident since, occurring as it did in the dark, it heightened the feeling of anxiety that something was wrong. Not only were we retiring, not only were some units of the Allied Army, to put it mildly, somewhat disorganised, but the enemy's patrols had been able to push through and snipe at our column. Who could say that this was not the beginning of a cavalry pursuit on a grand scale?

It says much for the discipline of the troops that, in spite of these disquieting events, their morale remained unimpaired, and the retreat was continued in perfect order. It was 1 a.m. before we got in.

On the 26th we started at 4 a.m., and marched viâ Priches to near La Groise, where we halted a long time. During the day we got news of an attack on some of the Guards Brigade at Landrecies the night before, in the course of which they had killed a great number of the enemy. This cheered up everyone a lot.

We had a quiet day and retired to Hannappes, where we arrived about 9 or 10 p.m., in pouring rain.

On the 27th we did not leave billets till about 7 a.m. We moved north-west, and the regiment was disposed of in some woods near Andigny. " A " Squadron had a patrol out under Lieut. Upton, who sent in news of German columns marching south-west beyond our left flank. " B " Squadron had one troop out under Lieut. Hall in the woods. Some of the enemy's patrols penetrated into the wood, and both squadrons had some casualties in encounters with them. Lieut. Upton sent in a message reporting having heard of some Belgian troops in, I think, Bussigny, and saying he was going to get in touch with them. The Colonel's remark on receiving this message was " He'll get scuppered."

These words proved only too true. The Belgians turned out to be Germans, and Lieut. Upton and one man spent four long years in captivity. Pte. Death escaped with a bullet through his rifle bucket. Lieut. Bairstow and a patrol of his were missing at the end of the day. We retired in the evening to Hauteville, and did what seemed a long march in the dark. By now we were getting used to this.

On the 28th we moved off much as usual about 4 a.m., and marched in a south-westerly direction down the valley of the Oise. Then we moved up on to the high ground near Cerizy to cover from the north the retirement of General Horne's infantry brigade, who were marching down the valley. This brigade in turn was covering the march of the remainder of the 1st Corps. "A" Squadron had been detached from the brigade, and was away from us all this day. Soon after reaching the high ground, stragglers from some French territorials who had been holding St. Quentin began to pass through us, retiring south along the road to La Fère. They told us that the Germans had attacked St. Quentin with guns and machine guns, of which they themselves had none, and had driven them out.

To meet any attack that might come from St. Quentin, our brigade was disposed as follows:—The Greys were on the right of the main St. Quentin—La Fère road, 20th on the left with orders to watch the left flank most particularly. The main road was inclusive to the 20th, the 12th Lancers were in reserve at Moy. "C" Squadron of ours were made responsible for the main road, Lieut. Goodhart being well forward in a farm on the right of the road, supported by Lieut. Sparrow. Captain Mangles kept his other two troops in hand. "B" Squadron had Lieut. Peploe's troop out guarding the left flank. The rest of the squadron was with Regimental Headquarters at a cross-roads, from which a very good view could be obtained of the country in front. Lieut. Peploe got in touch with some patrols of the 3rd Cavalry Brigade. These had had encounters with German cavalry patrols, and some 4th Hussars claimed to have stuck some Germans with their swords. After a bit German cavalry patrols appeared on the horizon, but they did not show much dash and cannot have found out very much. Lieut. Goodhart, however, was driven in on to the main position. An action presently developed on our right. Major Swettenham's squadron of the Greys was holding a long narrow wood just on the right of Captain Mangles' squadron. The German patrols had apparently found out that there was something in the wood, but they had probably no idea what was really there. I imagine that some German general behind became impatient, and told his advanced guard to push on. How often have we not seen this? Lord Macaulay, in his poem on the fable of Horatius, describes just such a scene when he tells us that "Those behind cried forward and those before cried back."

The German manœuvre was not quite what we had expected in modern war. What looked like a strong squadron suddenly galloped over the brow of the hill some 500 or 600 yards in front of Major Swettenham's position. They dismounted well down the forward slope, and opened fire from the standing position just in front of their horses; by now some of "J" battery were in action, and the 12th Lancers had come up from Moy, where they had been enjoying a bathe in a lake. The guns opened on the Germans, who also came in for some attention from the 12th Lancers' machine guns and rifles. The 12th had come into action on the enemy's left flank. The German horses stampeded, and very soon some of the men started waving white handkerchiefs in token of surrender. The 12th completed the job by charging the dismounted Germans with a squadron, supported by one squadron of the Greys. Before this, Major Swettenham was most unfortunately killed by a German bullet, though his squadron on the whole had very few casualties. When the Brigadier told the 12th and Greys to attack, he at the same time sent orders to the 20th to advance, keeping in touch with the Greys, and still guarding the left flank of the brigade. Just about this time, Colonel Edwards located a battery of German guns in action away to his left front. Realising that this battery might prove a serious menace to General Chetwode's main attack and to " J " Battery, who had certainly one section firing " over the sights " (and possibly even the whole battery), the Colonel immediately decided to attack the guns, with the object of putting them out of action if possible or, at any rate, of diverting their attention from the rest of our brigade. Lieut. Peploe, with the 1st troop of " B " Squadron, was ordered to guard the left flank. Lieut. Sparrow, with the 1st troop of " C " Squadron, to keep touch with the Greys. With the remaining six troops, the Colonel galloped forward to attack the guns. The three troops of " C " Squadron, under Captain Mangles, came into action dismounted about 400 yards from the German battery. Meanwhile, " B " Squadron were trying to find a way by which to make a mounted attack. This was difficult, owing to wire fences. Finding a mounted attack impracticable, the Colonel ordered Captain Little to retire with his squadron by a more or less covered route that existed on the left flank. Meanwhile, the attack certainly achieved the object of keeping the enemy's guns busy. They concentrated their fire on " C " Squadron. There were considerable casualties among the led horses, and very soon these had to retire to a covered position some way in rear.

The three troops remained in action dismounted in a root field, and continued to monopolise the attention of the German gunners.

Meanwhile, Lieut. Sparrow's troop had joined in on the left of the main attack, and several of his men had the satisfaction of getting home with their swords against some dismounted Germans. The French interpreter attached to the troop—by name Landier, though better known in the regiment as " Chirby "—achieved the ambition of every Frenchman by killing a Boche. He shot him with his revolver. He had every intention of sticking him with his sword, but it is recorded that his horse shied off three times. He must have had more than the regulation six inches from knee to knee from the rest of the troop. Finally, when " B " Squadron had got back to a position in rear, and when the Brigadier's main attack had succeeded, Captain Mangles withdrew his three troops to their horses. This proved a very unpleasant manœuvre, as they were under heavy shrapnel fire most of the way and were doubling up hill. The weather, too, was very hot. By the time " C " Squadron had got back to their horses, the brigade had begun to withdraw from the battlefield in the direction of billets, the 20th being detailed to cover the retirement. This took place without any interference from the enemy, " B " Squadron finally throwing out a rear party. A German patrol could be seen following up for a short distance, but they gave us no trouble and did not come on very far.

I have confined myself in the above description to the doings of the regiment without giving details of what the rest of the brigade did; as a matter of fact, the attack by the 12th Lancers was a very fine feat of arms. Colonel Wormald led the squadron in person. He himself is reported to have broken his sword in a German's body, and the Adjutant, Captain Bryant accounted for several of the enemy. The rank and file just took the Huns like pegs. The C.O. was wounded and the Squadron Leader, Captain Michell, was killed. As soon as the squadron had charged through the Germans, it was rallied by Lieut. Wyndham Quinn, who wheeled it about and charged back again, accounting for the few Germans remaining unwounded. He then rallied a second time, and collected five wounded prisoners. "Moy," or "Cerizy," as it is variously called, was a 12th Lancer battle. The 20th are, however, proud to have played a part, however small, in an engagement that at the moment provided the one bright spot in an otherwise very black page in the history of the war. This fight brings out several very useful lessons. Firstly, the futility of the German frontal reconnaissance. No effort was made to find out where our flanks rested or to see what was behind. Consequently, when the German attack was launched, it was against an enemy about whom nothing, or next to nothing, was known. The Boche probably expected to meet a beaten and demoralised foe; instead, he met a brigade of British cavalry that had not up till then been seriously engaged, a brigade longing for a smack at the enemy.

Secondly, there is much to learn from General Chetwode's dispositions. The protective reconnaissance was pushed well forward, thus giving early information of the enemy's movements. What troops were in position were admirably concealed. As large a force as possible was kept in reserve and was, therefore, available when it was wanted.

Lastly, an excellent example is provided of one way in which cavalry can fight a rear-guard action.

On the 24th August we had an example of a purely defensive action. On the 28th the enemy were more aggressive; indeed, it is probable that they were intoxicated with success. Full advantage was taken of their state of intoxication. They made a bad mistake; at exactly the right moment

Chapter II.

the Brigadier profited by this error, and delivered a smashing counter-attack.

This attack achieved its object, but was not pressed too far. While the enemy were still staggering under the blow they had received, the attacking troops were quickly and skilfully withdrawn. I may mention in this connection that the withdrawal was greatly facilitated by the action of " J " Battery, who " lifted " on to the German reserves, who might otherwise have interfered. We had a long ride back that night, some twenty-five miles, to our billets at Autreville.

Most of this was done in the dark, and it is no exaggeration to say that the majority of us slept soundly in our saddles as we rode along. During the moments of semi-consciousness, everyone was supremely happy. The day we had lived for had come—the British cavalry had got home with their lances and swords into the Huns. Our state of mind was very similar to that of a school football team driving home after a victorious encounter with a rival school who had always prided themselves that they were invincible. Our opponents on this day had been some Dragoons of the Guard.

Entering Chauny, where we crossed the Oise, the head of the regiment was suddenly challenged. The Colonel pulled old " Iris " up on her hocks, when he realised that a picket belonging to the Brigade of Guards had turned out and was drawn up across the road, with their bayonets at the " engage." Having established our identity we were allowed to proceed, and we certainly had a comfortable feeling that the bridge at Chauny was in safe keeping that night. The British Army had not been reduced to quite the rabble that " Fritz " was probably led to imagine. We reached billets some time after midnight, and were at once greeted with the news that we had got to find one squadron to go off as soon as possible on a job as a contact squadron. It was " A " Squadron's turn, but they had not yet rejoined, and we had no notion where they were. Arthur Little was warned that unless he could find " A," he must take his squadron.

Had it been humanly possible to find " A " Squadron, I think the O.C. " B " would have done it. He failed to find them, and poor old " B " had to go. The only people of " A " Squadron who were then present were Lieut. Bairstow's patrol that had been missing the night of the 27th and had rejoined during the day. "B" Squadron marched at 2.30 a.m. on the 29th. At first they were to go to Fargniers close to La-Fère, but finally they were sent farther north to reconnoitre towards Cerizy. It was a foggy morning, and to make things more difficult we were very short of maps, as we had retired further south than had ever been anticipated. Consequently, we had got off the maps issued on the outbreak of war. A very few others had been hastily collected and issued, but only one copy was available for the whole of "B" Squadron. This the Squadron Leader naturally kept.

Lieut. Hall's was the leading troop. That officer had a look at the map before starting, and then committed the country to memory. He encountered a chain of German cavalry standing patrols just south of Cerizy, but they appeared to be merely protective patrols and did not advance before the Squadron was withdrawn about midday. The 29th was to be a rest day, so reveillé was later than usual; we breakfasted and shaved in comfort, and also indulged in a wash, the first proper wash most of us had had for ten days. About noon the rest day came to an end, and we saddled up. The brigade moved north through Chauny. Rumour had it that we were going to the support of the 3rd Cavalry Brigade. We marched some six miles north of Chauny and then halted. The regiment being responsible for the protection of the brigade, put out standing patrols, and at least one of these got in touch with the 16th Lancers, but we got no news of the enemy. Some French troops were making a counter-attack somewhere to the northeast, and achieved a very considerable success. We returned in the evening to our billets of the night before at Autreville.

On the 30th the retreat was continued. The brigade acted as rearguard to an infantry column, and marched viâ St. Gobain, through the forest of that name, to Vauxaillon, where we went into billets. We neither saw nor heard anything of the enemy during the day. It will be noticed that whereas up to and including the 28th August we had daily been in touch with the enemy, we had now for two days seen nothing of him. It did not seem possible that we had marched at such a pace as to have altogether shaken off the pursuit. Now that we know the history of the war from the German side as well as our own, the reason for this is obvious. Up to and including the 27th, we had been opposed to the cavalry of Von Kluck's 1st Army. This had been the extreme right flank of the German line.

After the 27th, Von Kluck was engaged in a wide turning movement which took him a considerable distance to the west of the line of retreat of the British Army. The next German Army to the east was Von Bülow's 2nd Army. This Army was engaged with the French 5th Army on our right. The cavalry with whom we were engaged on the 28th belonged, I believe, to Von Bülow. Thus, there was a gap between the German 1st and 2nd Armies and, thanks to this gap, the British Army was allowed to go unpursued. The effects of this were far-reaching. By the evening of the 28th both our men and our horses were, to say the least of it, pretty tired. Rations and forage had, thanks to good organisation, been sufficient, but we were very short of sleep. It will be seen that the average " night " had brought us little more than two hours' actual rest, usually between about one and three a.m. During the day we had been kept pretty busy, even when we were not actually in action. During the 29th and 30th we had no anxiety concerning the enemy—consequently, although our nights were still short, we put in a good sleep in the middle of the day, the service of protection being entrusted to the smallest force compatible with safety. What was happening in our regiment was also happening throughout the British Army. On the evening of the 28th, the Army, though undefeated, was a very tired Army. The two following days of comparative quiet were sufficient to restore that Army to fine fighting trim. Reading the German account of this phase, it would seem that our enemy had over-estimated our exhaustion.

By the 27th, he considered us no longer worth bothering about. Instead of making a further effort to compass our destruction by vigorous pursuit, Von Kluck went off in pursuit of what had become to the German military mind almost a religion " envelopment." The history of the retreat shows how this envelopment failed, how Von Kluck then had to change his direction once more from south-west to south-east. The result was that when he again came in contact with the British rearguard, his Army had had to march along two sides of a triangle, while we merely retired along its base. Thus, when we next met, the German troops were considerably more exhausted than our own. I shall describe these encounters later. I have digressed from my immediate narrative at this point in order to account for our immunity from pursuit during the days in question.

On the 31st we did a real " peace march." We moved off at 9 a.m. on a glorious summer's day, and trekked along in a leisurely fashion, for all the world as though we were not at war at all. We crossed the Aisne below Soissons, and halted on the southern bank for two hours.

Horses were off-saddled, and we had a bathe in the river, which was much appreciated. We billeted that night at Dommiers and St. Pierre Aigle. We put out outposts, each regiment finding its own. News had come in that Von Kluck was once more in the offing. The transport was sent off in a hurry in the middle of the night, Captain Barne being put in charge of the Brigade " B " Echelon for the next day. Lieut. Thompson was in charge of the Brigade " A " Echelon.

We were really behind our infantry this night, yet the Brigadier took the extra precaution of making his brigade responsible for their own safety. Though the night passed quietly, it is interesting to note that it was during this very night, at least during the early hours of the 1st September, that the 1st Cavalry Brigade were surprised in their billets at Néry by an equally surprised force of the enemy. Outpost duty is irksome and tiring, but there is a golden rule in the drill book to the effect that " every body of troops is responsible for its own protection." To neglect this rule is to court trouble. As a matter of fact, the 1st Brigade put up a very good show at Néry, discomfited the enemy, and captured a battery of guns.

Early in the morning of 1st of September, patrols were sent out under Lieut. Hall and Lieut. Sparrow to watch the crossings over the Aisne and report if the Germans got across. The bridges were believed to have been destroyed. Reports were to be sent to St. Pierre Aigle. If the brigade had left that place, it could be presumed that they were moving on Villers Cotterets. At about 10 a.m., the regiment was detached from the rest of the brigade, and placed under the orders of General Maxse, whose infantry brigade was the rearguard of the 1st Division. The day's march lay through the Fôret de Retz, which made the task of finding suitable rearguard positions a very difficult one. Our first position was about one mile south-east of St. Pierre Aigle. Here there was a bit of high ground devoid of trees rising up in the middle of the woods. It was a bad position, but there was no better one available. Fortunately, we were not attacked, and fell back soon after midday to some cross-roads in the centre of the forest about four miles north-east of Villers Cotterets on the Villers Cotterets-Soissons road. Here Regimental Headquarters and " B " Squadron were established. ' A " Squadron were on the left and " C " Squadron on the right, guarding all roads and tracks leading west, north and east.

While we were holding this position, Lieut. Hall's patrol rejoined, having had quite an exciting time. Their orders had been to watch the river crossings near Ambleny. They reached that place about 6 a.m., after passing through our infantry outposts at Coeuvres.

The infantry reported a quiet night, and at Ambleny there was no sign of the enemy. The patrol then left the road and climbed the hill just to the north-west of the village. Here they established themselves in a position from which they had a very good view of the Aisne valley, and particularly of the bridge at Le Port. This was the crossing that it was their special duty to watch. About 7.30 a.m., large columns of German troops could be seen across the Aisne about Nouvron moving south, that is, towards the river. At 9 a.m., a squadron of German cavalry crossed the bridge and advanced along the Ambleny road. The original orders of the patrol had been to remain in observation of the river until midday. Lieut. Hall, however, appreciated and, I think, appreciated rightly that the time had come to retire.

He had gained valuable information : (1) That the enemy had got an intact bridge at Le Port; (2) that they were in strength just north of the river. If he stayed where he was he could not find out much more—also, it was important to get this information to St. Pierre Aigle before the German squadron that had crossed got into a position to intercept the message. The patrol rode down the hill towards Ambleny. Just as they were approaching the road, a car full of German officers passed, coming from the *south*. The patrol were all on their horses, and the car was travelling fast, also both sides were taken completely by surprise at such an encounter. They therefore merely cursed each other in their respective languages as the car flashed by. This incident, however, showed Lieut. Hall that the Germans must have crossed the Aisne at some other place besides Le Port, and made him realise that the task of rejoining the regiment, and getting his information to them, was not going to be so simple as he had thought.

He retired to Coeuvres, which he found unoccupied. Here he wrote his report, which he sent by an orderly to St. Pierre Aigle, expecting that the regiment would still be there. At the same time he laid a neat little ambush at the southern end of Coeuvres, in case any more Hun motor cars should come along. The orderly returned after a bit, saying that he had been unable to reach his destination, as he had met a squadron of German cavalry moving from St. Pierre Aigle towards Coeuvres. Lieut. Hall then gave the order to mount, and moved off to try and rejoin the regiment somewhere in the Forêt de Retz.

It was obvious that they must have retired from St. Pierre Aigle, and probable that the C.O. already knew that the enemy had crossed the Aisne. Thus, the only thing remaining to be done was to get the patrol back safe and sound. They moved across country, marching in a south-westerly direction. Before very long, they came on unmistakable signs of a rearguard action, broken rifles, blood-stained clothing, etc., and identified some of it as belonging to an Irish battalion that they had seen at Coeuvres early that morning. This made it look rather as though the enemy had crossed in force somewhere, and were already between the patrol and the regiment. Some trouble might be experienced in getting through them. The day was very hot, and the horses were tired after several days of continuous marching, fighting and patrolling. They could only just raise a trot. The village of Soucy was presently found to be occupied by Germans, and on the high ground to the south a battle was in progress. The German advanced guard were attacking some British infantry, who appeared to be fighting with their usual gallantry against what seemed to be greatly superior numbers. The patrol then made for Montgobert, but

Chapter II.

were at that moment spotted by a German cavalry patrol. The latter were about 400 yards away to the west, and, bringing their lances to the engage, started to charge. Lieut. Hall's rear point was Pte. Hayhurst, who, as Corporal Hayhurst, was unfortunately killed near Vermelles in 1916. This gallant soldier, for such he always was, at once drew his sword, turned about, and charged towards the Germans alone. This unlooked-for attack, though made by a single man only, seems to have disconcerted the Huns. They wheeled about and retired to Soucy at a gallop. Pte. Hayhurst quietly rejoined his patrol. This was a fine exhibition of the cavalry spirit which reaped its almost invariable reward. The patrol reached Mont-Gobert all right, and threaded their way cautiously through the village. They got through without meeting a soul, and there before them lay stretched the great Fôret de Retz. There were several bodies of German cavalry to be seen short of the woods, but Lieut. Hall decided to ride boldly through them, trusting they would mistake his patrol for one of their own. In this he was completely successful, and reached the forest without arousing the enemy's suspicions. The forest was like most French forests—the undergrowth was fairly thick, and it was intersected by long, straight rides which crossed each other at right angles. A map is usually quite unreliable in such places, so Lieut. Hall put his in his pocket and marched due south by the sun. He kept off the rides, and in fact chose some of the thickest undergrowth as his line of march, for he quite expected that the enemy would have penetrated into the forest. He was leading the patrol himself, when suddenly he became aware of a man in front of him. He left his horse and stalked him, revolver in hand. When he got to point-blank range, he found it was a sentry of " A " Squadron. In his own description of the encounter, he says : " Although he had a week's growth of beard, I thought he was the best thing I had seen since I left England."

Lieut. Sparrow's patrol rejoined about the same time. They had been sent to watch the river crossing at Vic sur Aisne. They found a good position on high ground, much the same as Lieut. Hall's patrol did, and very soon saw some German cavalry cross. About a troop of Germans approached a position held by Sergt. Goodwin and a few men. These opened a heavy fire, and the Huns beat a hasty retreat. It is possible that they thought there really was a force of some size in position. Anyway, they did not make any other attempt to advance. No more Germans crossed at Vic, but Lieut. Sparrow was able to observe large numbers crossing at Le Port. He at once sent in a report on the situation to the Colonel at St. Pierre Aigle. Eventually, he fell back on the Fôret de Retz. He had some difficulty in getting through. After skirting a village which was full of Germans, he met a party of our infantry marching north. The officer in command told him he could not go south, as there were Huns there. Lieut. Sparrow replied that there were also Huns to the north. History does not relate what happened to the infantry. On such occasions it is better to be mounted than on foot. Assisted by a good eye for country and a bit of luck, Lieut. Sparrow got his men back all right.

During the late afternoon, an attack by Jaegers and cyclists began to develop against " A " Squadron. " C " were, I think, opposed by patrols only. Our infantry had by now reached Villers Cotterets, and, owing to the pressure on our left flank, the C.O. issued orders to retire towards that place. It took some little time to collect " C " Squadron. The Squadron Leader was himself engaged at the moment in stalking a German patrol, and was quite annoyed at having his sport interfered with by the order to retire. The next thing we knew was that the Germans had outflanked the left of " A " Squadron, crossed the Villers Cotterets road, and entered the woods on our left rear. We had discharged our duty so far as General Maxse's Brigade was concerned, for at Villers Cotterets they had rejoined the remainder of their Division. The next problem was how to extricate the regiment. We had no road left by which to retire, so we struck off along a boggy forest track, merely leading south-west by the sun. The only wheels accompanying us were the machine gun limbers. These experienced difficulty, but got through somehow. " A " Squadron acted as rearguard to the regiment till " C " had got by. They did it very well, and, by well-judged bursts of fire, prevented the enemy from pressing us, and probably made him think the opposition was more serious than it really was. " A " Squadron had Sergt. Cook wounded,

Chapter II.

but got him away, though the poor fellow had a very rough time of it remaining in the saddle, as he was suffering a lot of pain and was feeling pretty bad. However, he stuck it well on his good little mare, A.16, on which he had won the Sergeants' Light-Weight Point to Point. The cavalryman's devotion to his horse was exemplified when this N.C.O. reached an ambulance. He was told the mare was going to be taken for some officer to ride, and would not be returned to the regiment. Wounded as he was, he escaped from the ambulance, recovered the mare, and rejoined his squadron! We continued our march through the forest till we struck the Villers Cotterets-La Ferté Milon road. We followed this road, and at Bourgfontaine Farm found the rest of the brigade. After waiting there some time, we withdrew to our billets, or rather bivouac at La Villeveuve, getting in about 11 p.m. September 2nd was a quiet day. We saddled up at 3 a.m., but waited at the brigade rendezvous, which was just outside La Villeveuve, till 9 a.m. I think the 12th were leading regiment, and so were responsible for protection. Anyway, we were not, so we put in some good sleep, making ourselves comfortable among some sheaves of corn, for the corn was all cut but had not been carried. About 9 a.m., we began a leisurely march via May-en-Mutien and Vareddes to Trilport, where we crossed to the south bank of the Marne. On the way we came upon a large ration dump that had been left the night before for some brigade, who had never found it. We loaded ourselves with what we wanted, and, I think, with probably more than we required, and then burnt the rest. It made a fine blaze, and anyway the Boche didn't get it.

The regiment spent the night at Trilport, "C" Squadron occupying the bridges at Mary and Lizy-sur-Ourcq. They were not attacked. The next morning, 3rd September, the brigade crossed to the north of the Marne at Changis. We took up a defensive position on the high ground west of Avernes to protect the flank of an infantry column, who were marching south through La Ferté-sous-Jouarre, against any attack that might come from the west or north-west. "C" Squadron had crossed the river at Mary, and took up an outpost position on a hill to the east of that village.

From there they could watch the country north-west of

the Ourcq, and also the ground east of that river and due north of their position. Lieut. Sparrow's troop occupied the crossing over the Ourcq at Lizy-sur-Ourcq. Soon after midday German patrols began to appear on the ground east of the Ourcq. Lieut. Sparrow opened fire on them and checked them. About 3 p.m., however, a considerable force of cavalry with some guns could be seen approaching the squadron's main position from the north. Lieut. Sparrow was in danger of being cut off, and was withdrawn. The German guns opened fire on the squadron and caused some casualties, including Corporal Garness, who was killed.

The position of the squadron was very exposed, so Capt. Mangles withdrew to Jaignes, where he dismounted and awaited the enemy's attack. The Germans dismounted some way off and attacked the village on foot. The squadron were able to fire at them at about 600 yards, and delayed their attack considerably. Eventually finding his flanks were getting turned, and being unsupported, Captain Mangles mounted his squadron and effected another retirement of about 1,000 yards.

This was done under shrapnel fire, but no casualties resulted. " C " Squadron had delayed the enemy so well that the time had now come when the brigade could withdraw south of the Marne. This they did, crossing the river at Ussy. " B " Squadron were sent forward to cover the retirement of " C," and " J " Battery also came into action. In making their final retirement, " B " Squadron had several men killed, including Captain Cristy, whose death lost us a very good officer. The last man to cross the river was Colonel Edwards himself. He stayed behind with nothing between him and the enemy until he was perfectly satisfied that a patrol of about three men that had been sent out had been withdrawn. Incidents such as this endeared him to all the men. They were always certain that wherever they were sent, they would not be forgotten. This fact contributed, I think, considerably to the boldness with which our patrols always acted. As soon as we had crossed, the bridge was blown up, and there was no more interference from the enemy. In skirting La Ferté we passed through our infantry in their billets. We ourselves marched south for another four miles and bivouacked near Rue-de-Vrou. Perhaps the drill book would call it " close billets." The lucky ones found barns to sleep in, the others slept in the open.

We thought we should be left in peace for a bit the next morning, as all the bridges over the Marne should have been destroyed.

To make doubly sure, three officers' patrols from the regiment, found by "A" Squadron, were sent out at about 4.30 a.m. These patrols were commanded by Lieuts. Bairstow, Galbraith and Silvertop. It was a foggy morning. The patrols were all to go to crossings over the Marne.

They had all encountered the enemy by 6 a.m., and Lieut. Bairstow was severely wounded at Courcelles, about two miles from our bivouac.

A late start had been intended, but, owing to these events, the brigade saddled up in a hurry. We moved off at about 9 a.m., and occupied a rearguard position. Regimental and Brigade Headquarters were at Doue, with squadrons disposed as follows :—" A " Squadron and M.G. close at hand; " B " at Soulsoy; " C " at Montgoins.

Some German patrols approached " C " Squadron's position, but the squadron was well concealed, and Captain Mangles was most careful to withhold his fire. Consequently, the enemy could not find out very much, and did not like to risk an attack. The 4th troop of " C " (Lieut. Goodhart) had a shoot at a German motor cyclist at a range of 50 yards. He turned about and escaped! Perhaps there was, after all, some justification for the notice scribbled on the wall in the butts at Lydd, a good many years ago, by some facetious marker: " Haldane diddled, or how ' C ' Squadron got their Service pay." " B " Squadron became engaged with German patrols, but were not seriously attacked. About 2 p.m., just as German troops could be seen getting out of motor 'buses and deploying for an attack, the regiment was ordered to concentrate round Doue. The Greys and 12th Lancers had already retired. We then took up a rearguard position at Doue. This was held till 3.30, when we were ordered to retire on the rest of the brigade. The retirement was covered by " B " Squadron and the Machine Gun Section, who took up a strong position on the hill by the church at Doue, and got shelled as they were leaving. " J " Battery also let off a few rounds to steady the Huns. Afterwards, the retirement of the main body was not interfered with, though " A " Squadron, who had now become rearguard, were fighting a series of rearguard actions as long as daylight lasted. We fell back through Coulommiers. The infantry outposts at that place were attacked during the night, but repulsed the enemy. We spent the night at Le Puits, a few miles further south.

The following day (5th September) we made a further retirement via Rozoy to bivouac at Sëgres. It is recorded in Myles Thompson's diary that there he slept in a bed, for the first time in the war.

This was the end of the retreat. For the last day or two there had been rumours that the tide was going to turn. Tales got about that the enemy were being drawn on into a bottle-neck position, the British Army being the cork. All this turned out in the end to be more or less true, an unusual thing for rumours of the kind. The troops against whom we had been engaged during the last few days were chiefly Von Marwitz's Cavalry Corps. This corps was guarding the right flank of the German 1st Army (Von Kluck) during his march south-east to attack the French 5th Army. News got about that we were to turn round and advance the next day. This was hailed with joy, though no one knew the reason for it. It is now an historical fact that the reason was this : When Von Kluck turned south-east, he left one corps (the 4th reserve) to watch the new French 6th Army that had been forming on the British left. As this 6th Army grew in strength, so the Germans became unable to hold them, and Von Kluck had to abandon his attack on the 5th Army and retrace his steps in order to help his 4th reserve corps. Had this corps been defeated and broken, he would have been cut off. When he decided on his retirement to the north, he left Von Marwitz's Cavalry Corps to keep the British in check. It was against part of this corps that we were fighting during the period known as the battle of the Marne. I have outlined these facts so as to show how the experiences of the regiment fit in with the general run of events as they are now known to history. It is thus seen how we played our little part in the great drama that was then being enacted. I will pause at this point to review the retreat as a whole, as it affected us.

Chapter II.

It is well known that during this retreat many, I might say nearly all, units of the British Army got at one time or another pretty severely handled. Yet, in writing this account, which is, I hope, fairly accurate, I have not described a single action in which the brigade were what might be called seriously engaged, except at Cerizy, which was a brilliant success. Even on that day, the Brigadier always had at least two squadrons still in hand. How is this to be accounted for? Did we always run away when danger threatened? Scarcely —the infantry whom we were protecting never suffered any interference from the enemy. We were never even engaged at all close on the top of them.

Were we lucky in always striking a "cooshy" part of the battlefield? Partly, I admit. Still, there is one fact that stands out. Constantly we find that a German attack was developing just as the time had come for us to retire, or that we retired just as an attack was developing. This is the very essence of a rearguard action—to make the enemy deploy, thus wasting his time; then, when he has made his maximum deployment, to slip away, thus causing him further delay in reforming column of route. For the fact that we succeeded over and over again in successfully playing this game with very few casualties to ourselves, credit is due to the skill with which the brigade, regiments and squadrons were posted and handled before and during the action. It is also due in a very large measure to the excellence of the work done by the officers' patrols. These small bodies of men, who were usually pushed boldly out a long way in advance of the main position, not only gave that "early information of the enemy's movements" on which the drill book insists, but also by their bold action must have caused our enemy delay and inconvenience out of all proportion to their numerical strength.

In considering the part played by the British Army as a whole at Mons and during the retreat, it is interesting to note a passage from the pen of General Von Moltke, Chief of the German General Staff in 1914. In some reminiscences of his that have lately been published by his widow appears the following:—"That the complete defeat of France in our first advance did not come off is due to the rapid assistance brought to her by England."

CHAPTER III.—The Marne and Aisne.

ON the 6th of September, we saddled up at 4 a.m., and started off, this time heading north. Consequently everyone was in the best of spirits. The 20th were the leading regiment of the brigade, "A" Squadron finding the advanced guard. We halted for some time south of the Bois de Lumigny, near some heavy guns which seemed to have a target of some sort. They were doing a good bit of firing, anyway. Meanwhile, the 12th Lancers became engaged with the enemy at Ormeaux, and "B" Squadron were sent to their support. "B" did not actually come into action, although they got shelled and lost five men. The 12th captured a German motor car. They kept it with the regiment for some time, finding a man to drive it, and it proved very useful to them, till at last orders were issued that all such little trophies must be handed over to higher authority. We next moved to Marles and finally to Chateau-de-Lumigny for the night. Here we bivouacked in the chateau grounds. It was the first night in the war when not a soul in the regiment was under cover. However, it was a most perfect night and a very good bivouac, much healthier, I am sure, than some of the musty houses we had slept in. It had been an uneventful day, but anyway the advance had started. We had finished up about four miles further north than the night before, and stories were afloat that the Germans were taking a proper knock.

The next morning (7th September), we moved off about 6 a.m. I think it was this day that we settled to lighten the waggons for the pursuit. All the picks and shovels were thrown away. Signalling equipment was at one moment jettisoned, but the signalling officer managed to get it back on the waggon when no one was looking. There came a time later when we should have been glad of the picks and shovels. To this I shall come in due course. I think the preparations for a

Chapter III.

rapid pursuit were carried to excess. G.S. waggons are meant to move at a walk with the heavy baggage. They are not intended to pursue at a gallop like the chariots of Boadicea. Such men as Pte. Press and other transport drivers were not fashioned by nature to become "Jehus"; no more was Lieut. and Quartermaster Bill Adams, who had charge of "B" Echelon. So long as no unauthorised impedimenta are allowed on the waggons (later on gramophones had a way of getting there), and officers' valises do not exceed the stipulated weight, the transport will get along quite fast enough. We marched this day via Mauperthuis, Chailly and Charcot to Rebais. A certain number of German stragglers were met with and mopped up. Lieut. Sparrow shot a Hun cyclist with his revolver. During the afternoon, "C" Squadron were acting as right flank guard. They met some patrols of Uhlans, who fell back as we approached. At one place some delay was caused to the squadron by one of the advanced points being shot dead from a house covering a bridge. The Boches had cleared out by the time the house and bridge were in our hands. Shortly after this, Corpl. Goring killed two Uhlans and captured their lances, fine trophies. I fancy that he managed to smuggle them on to a transport waggon and eventually got them home to England, to show future generations of Gorings what father did in the Great War! We got to Rebais just after the Germans had left. An officer's patrol of the Greys had previously been ambushed there, and most of them, including the officer, killed. The enemy had looted most of the houses, furniture was strewn all about the streets, and some of the houses were burning. There were also dead horses lying about, killed by shrapnel. It was a scene typical of what history has taught us to expect in the wake of a retreating army. We went into close billets just outside Rebais, and put out night outposts.

The next day (8th September), we started at about 5 a.m., and advanced as far as the Petit Morin. Short of this we came under artillery fire. "J" Battery replied, and got a target at German cavalry across the stream. Our patrols reported that the crossings over the river were strongly occupied by the enemy. We waited on the south side of the river while an infantry brigade came up to make an attack. They did not make very rapid progress. We actually never advanced again that day, and eventually returned to billets near Rebais. I have never been able to reconcile the doings of this day with a vigorous pursuit of a retiring enemy. I think that at that particular spot we played the enemy's game. He was out to delay us with a rearguard, and he succeeded in doing so throughout a whole day. Probably we were unduly cautious in tackling an enemy before whom we had been retiring for so long. There may have been excellent reasons for our not getting on faster, but I do not believe the Germans were really in great strength. On the morning of the 9th, we continued our advance, and found that the infantry had secured the line of the Petit Morin and captured prisoners and machine guns. We marched via Le Tretoire and Boitron to the Marne, the crossings of which had already been secured by the infantry. We crossed by a bridge of boats between Nogent and Saulchery. At the latter place we halted for two hours. We then continued north, and eventually went into billets at Domptin. During the afternoon, Field Marshal Sir John French rode up, and went round addressing each regiment of the brigade in turn, saying what good work the cavalry had done during the retreat. We resumed the pursuit at about 3 a.m. on 10th September. We were leading regiment, " B " Squadron finding the advanced guard, and sending out patrols under Lieuts. Peploe, Carew and Hall. We entered Marigny not long after the Germans had left; then pushed on through a wood and up a long hill. " B " Squadron encountered some German stragglers in the wood, but soon cleared it and gained the northern edge.

" C " Squadron had meanwhile been sent off to the right flank, so we were really working on a two squadron front. On getting out of the wood we saw in a hollow below us a village, Veuilly, from which what looked like a convoy were trekking out. Captain Little sent forward a patrol, who very soon reported that they were Germans with an infantry escort.

We then saw a regiment of German cavalry retiring at a gallop over the skyline a mile or two away. Had we had support, I think we could have scuppered the Huns in Veuilly pretty quickly from the position that " C " Squadron were occupying. As it was, we heard at this moment that the rest of the

Chapter III.

brigade had been switched off to the left. This appeared to make it necessary to keep " A " and " B " Squadrons in their original position, so as not to make a still bigger gap in our line. An infantry brigade very soon came up and started an attack on Veuilly, supported by some field artillery. Personally, I think this would have been the moment to support " C " Squadron with the other two squadrons, so as to turn the enemy's left and even cut him off completely. I don't think it would have been a difficult manœuvre, and it would probably have meant that Veuilly would have been cleared much quicker than it was.

As it was, this proved a slow job. The German infantry, who had no guns to support them, fought well. Eventually, I think the whole lot were killed or captured. The Greys and 12th Lancers had advanced on the left, and had been in action in some woods in the hollow. One squadron (Major Fane's) of the 12th had brought off a charge against some more or less demoralised German infantry.

The 3rd Cavalry Brigade, under General Hubert Gough, appeared on our left, the two brigades coming under his orders. We all finally rallied on a hill, the far side of the valley, and continued the advance to Marizy-St. Mard, a village just south of the Ourcq.

We saw no more of the enemy the whole day. His method of fighting a rearguard action seems to have been to withdraw his mounted troops and artillery, and to leave some infantry to delay us as long as possible, making up his mind to sacrifice these. Perhaps they were told to hold certain places, such as Veuilly, till further orders, and then were deliberately not sent any further orders.

Anyway, they certainly did succeed in causing great delay to the pursuing force, though I imagine this method was more costly in killed, wounded and prisoners than was the method we employed in our retreat from Mons. I believe in other parts of the field rearguards of cavalry and Jaegers were encountered, but I can only speak of our experiences in the small bit of the front that we saw.

The following day we started about 5 a.m., and marched viâ Chouy and Billy-sur-Ourcq to Hartennes. We halted here for some time in heavy rain, and got very wet and cold. Then we went off to support the 3rd Cavalry Brigade, who had found some Boches and were in action. We did not become engaged and went back into billets for the night at Parcy Tigny. The whole regiment got into one huge farm—a very good place, too.

Next day (12th September), we marched via Hartennes, Chacrise and Ciry, to just south of Chassemy. The 3rd Cavalry Brigade were attacking Brenelle, the 1st Cavalry Brigade having already secured Braine. We were about to join in the attack on Brenelle when the garrison surrendered. They were pretty well surrounded, and were being bombarded by the 3rd Cavalry Brigade R.H.A. at very short range. The prisoners taken were all infantry. Most of them appeared to be oldish men. Optimists gaily announced that the Huns were getting short of man power, and were already throwing in their last reserve. Yet the war went on for another four years! We were now in possession of the heights overlooking the Aisne from the south. We retired to billets at Braine, the outposts on the high ground being taken over by some infantry.

At Braine we met Captain Rex Osborne, Staff Captain, 1st Cavalry Brigade. He told us how Major Cawley had been killed in the 1st Brigade fight at Néry on 1st September. He was also surprised to find that some food he had collected for his brigade and left lying about somewhere in Braine had disappeared.

He was more pained than angry when he discovered that it had been consumed by his own regiment. However, Heaven helps those who help themselves; and I don't suppose he left stuff lying about again.

This was the end of our share in the Battle of the Marne. It seems curious to note that we never heard of this battle until it was over. Yet we had been more or less engaged in it, and it will certainly prove to be one of the most important battles in history.

The fact is the heavy fighting was going on to our left and right. Where we were we encountered only German rearguards. We were covering a pretty wide front ourselves for the troops available. That is probably the reason why the pursuit was not more vigorous, and why we did not become engaged in any pitched battles. The issue of the battle was, I suppose, really decided on the left in the very heavy fighting that resulted

Chapter III.

in the French 6th Army driving back the German 1st Army, and on the right, where General Foch, commanding the 9th Army, delivered his historic counter-attack with his 42nd Division. Both these events took place on 9th September, and were probably greatly facilitated by the forcing of the Marne by the British Army.

For the 13th we were ordered to continue the pursuit, on the assumption that the enemy were not holding the line of the river Aisne. It was soon discovered that this assumption was wrong. Consequently, the attack was handed over to the infantry, and we returned to our billets at Braine. The infantry gained a footing on the north bank of the river. On this day the 3rd and 5th Cavalry Brigades were formed into the 2nd Cavalry Division under General Gough.

For the 14th, orders were again issued to cross the river and take up the pursuit. Vailly Bridge was named as the rendezvous for the brigade and the transport. The 20th were rear regiment of the brigade, so when we reached the bridge the Greys and 12th were already in Vailly. The bridge itself had been destroyed, but the R.E. had erected a pontoon alongside. It was found that the infantry had not gained the high ground north of the Aisne, as had at first been supposed, but they were in action just beyond the village.

The whole valley, including the bridge, was under hostile observation and artillery fire. It was a misty morning, and to this alone could be attributed the fact that we had got so far without drawing the enemy's fire. As the regiment reached the bridge the fog lifted, the German gunners spotted us and started firing. Pontoons are not intended to carry cavalry at a trot, at least this one was not, so the Colonel dismounted the regiment and gave the order to lead over in single file. This we did. As soon as we got into Vailly the position of our infantry became known, and the Brigadier ordered an immediate retirement over the bridge. Once more we had to face the ordeal of leading over in single file under heavy shell fire.

By now the Boche had got the range pretty well, and it became a very unpleasant manœuvre, especially for the last squadron, "B." The marvel is that we did not lose more men. The total casualties in the regiment were only ten, and these included the transport, who were also shelled about

Chassemy. By the time our last troop was across, the fire had become so heavy that the 12th and Greys were kept in Vailly till the afternoon, and then sent back by troops.

Even so, their casualties were heavier than ours. Eventually, the 3rd and 5th Brigades withdrew from the valley viâ Brenelle, making what use we could of the woods on the slope to conceal ourselves. A few shells dropped near us, but no damage was done.

We went into billets at Augy, and never moved far all the next day. The battle of the Aisne had now begun in earnest, and with it had commenced trench warfare. In this we were not called on to take part, except that on the 16th " C " Squadron and the Machine Gun Section were sent to hold the crossing over the Vesle, between Ciry and Condé. Here the squadron entrenched themselves, assisted by the R.E. They were withdrawn at 7 a.m. on the 17th. They had come under fire from Condé bridge, and had sustained one casualty, Pte. Dawson, killed, also a few horses.

The rôle of the 2nd Cavalry Division from now on was to send detachments to watch Condé Bridge, which was still in the enemy's hands. Just here there was a gap between our 3rd and 5th Divisions. This duty did not again fall to the regiment.

On the 17th a reinforcement of 63 men and 59 horses under Lieut. Moule (14th Hussars) and Lieut. Heap joined. Lieut. Moule went to " A " Squadron and Lieut. Heap to " B " Squadron.

On the 19th, as things seemed quiet, we were withdrawn to Lesges, where we had very comfortable billets. Here Lieut. Dodgson joined, and went to " A " Squadron. The only other excitement during the battle of the Aisne was on Sunday, 27th, when a message was suddenly received in the early morning to the effect that the enemy were crossing Condé Bridge " in large numbers," and the brigade was to assemble at once. We assembled. As a practice for an alarm, it was very useful.

The report was totally untrue, and after Divine Service we returned to billets.

On the 29th the Greys had some sports. A team of ours, coached by Lieut. and Quartermaster Bill Adams, won the tug-of-war open to the brigade, beating teams much heavier than themselves.

On the 30th, the brigade was withdrawn further from the Aisne, as a preliminary to marching north into Flanders to join in the movement that was intended to turn the enemy's right flank.

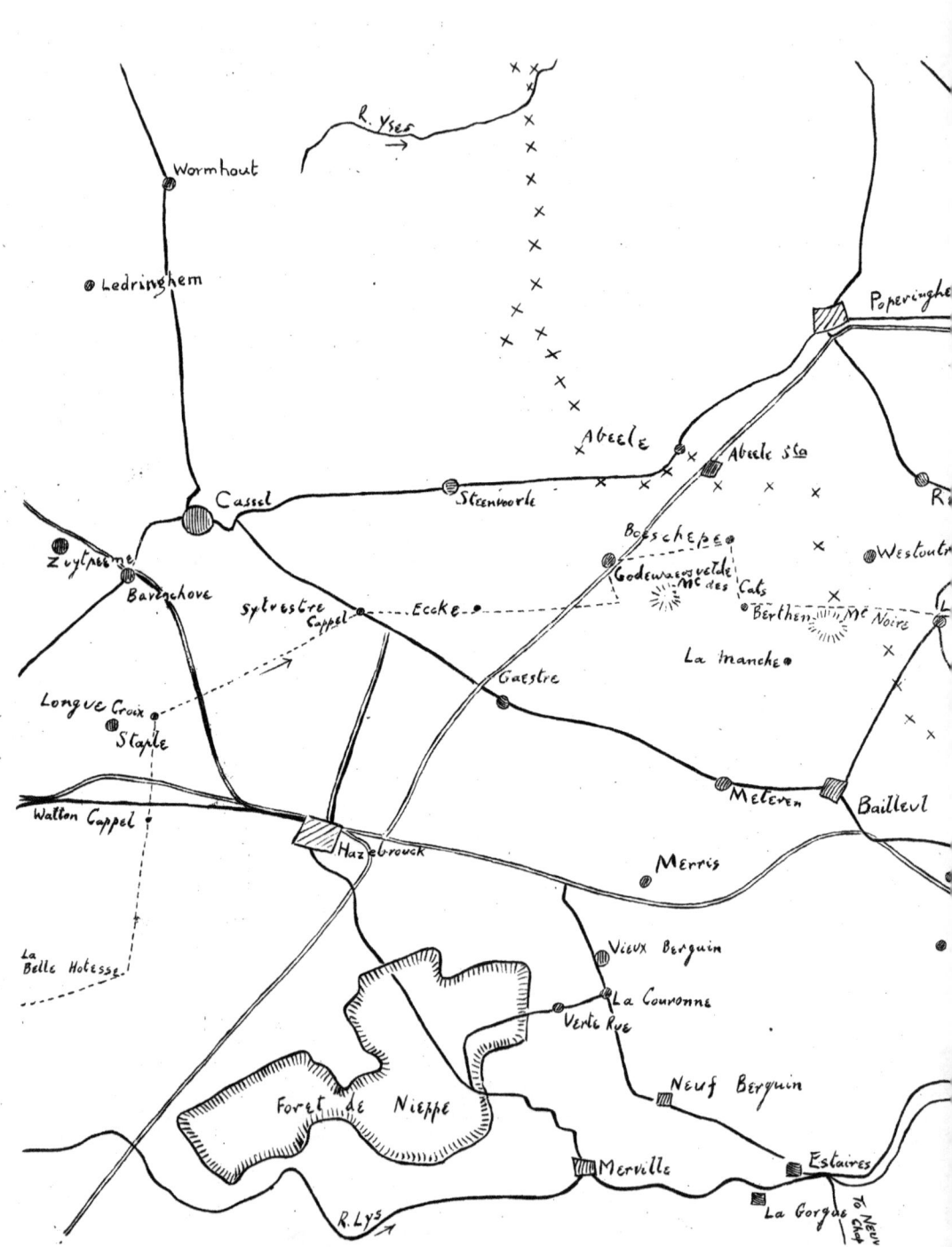

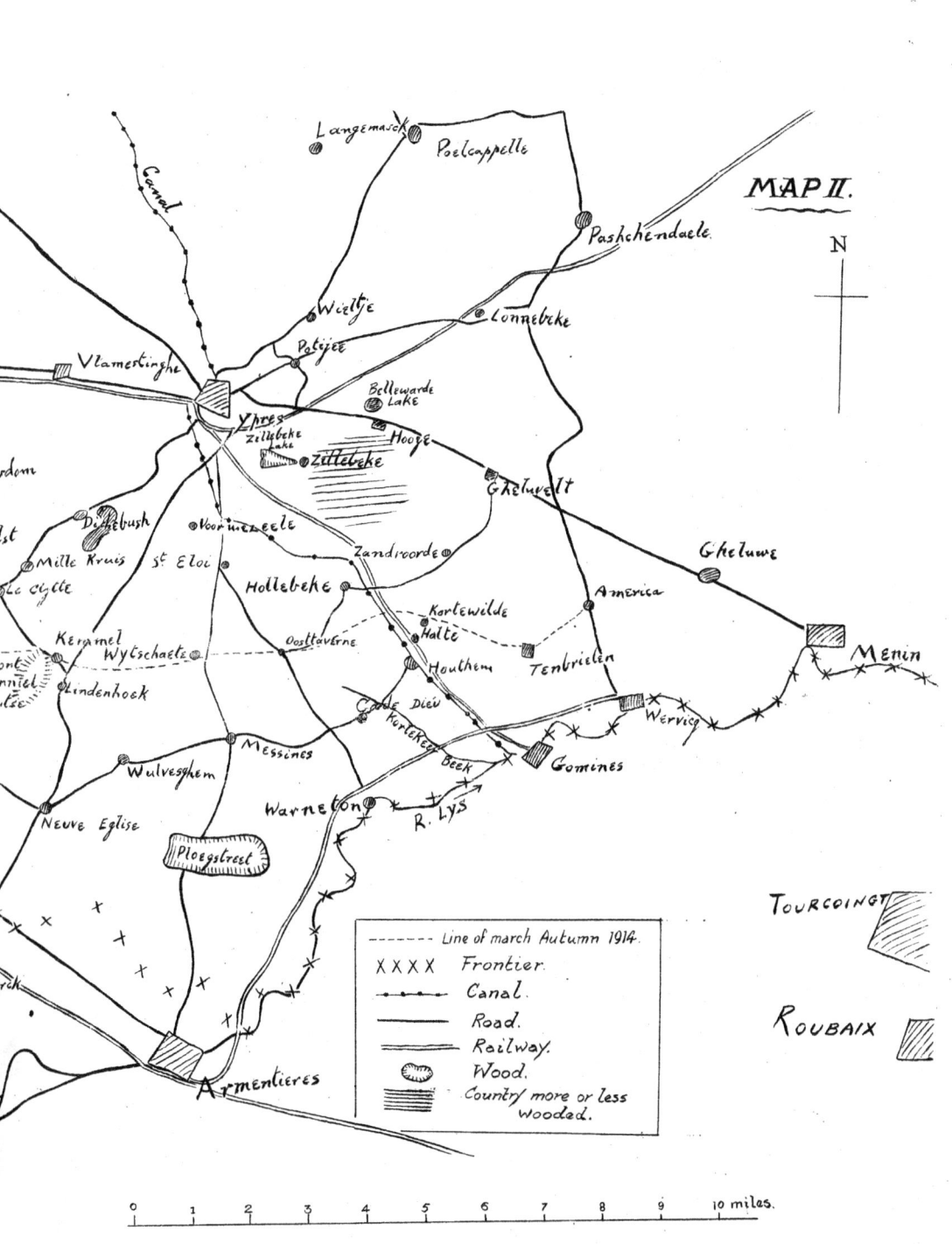

CHAPTER IV.—The First Battle of Ypres.

(See Maps I & II.)

THE progress of the war at this point is now well-known. Trench warfare had started along the Aisne, and soon extended from Soissons, pretty well without interruption, to the Swiss frontier.

General Joffre tried to turn this position from the west, and at about this time a French Army under General De Castelnau was making an attack about Roye. It was then decided, at the suggestion of Sir John French, to withdraw the British Army from the Aisne and once more bring it into line on the left of the Allied forces, thus simplifying the supply services viâ the Channel ports. This movement was also in the nature of yet another attempt to turn the German flank; for General De Castelnau had met strong German forces and was engaged in heavy fighting. Our two cavalry divisions moved by road, the infantry by rail. The 2nd Cavalry Division moved a day's march ahead of the 1st Cavalry Division. We marched by easy stages, the billeting areas each night being :— 30th September, Arcy St. Restitue; 1st October, Oulchy-la-Ville; 2nd, Marolles; 3rd, Raray; 4th, Méry; 5th and 6th, Mailly. Our march was arrested here for twenty-four hours, as it was thought that the French might need our help near Roye. Indeed, the regiment went up and gave a little " moral support," but were not needed further, and returned to Mailly.

I think it was while we were here that we heard that S.S.M. Wyborn of " B " Squadron, S.S.M. Hatton of " A " Squadron, and Sergt. Poole of " C " Squadron, had been given commissions. Hatton had been promoted S.S.M. vice Morwood, 2nd Lieut. Wyborn went to " A," 2nd Lieut. Poole to " B," and 2nd Lieut. Hatton to " C." It is unfortunate that it was at this place, where we were spending two nights, that the signalling officer, who did the billeting, chose, from purely tactical considerations, a schoolhouse devoid of furniture as the Headquarter Mess. This was the more galling as one of the squadrons, "B," I think, had a "château." After this it became Major Cook's duty to select headquarters each night.

On the 7th we marched through Amiens and billeted just north of the town. It froze hard that night, and very cold it was when we started next morning. The 8th we slept at Domqueur, the 9th at Humières and the 10th at Rombly. This day a patrol had been as far as Aire, and had effected a liaison with the French territorials who were holding the town. The patrol had a tremendous reception from the inhabitants; and the territorials were much relieved on hearing that the British Army was at hand. They had a long front to hold and had no artillery. German cavalry were reported to be in the Forêt de Nieppe. French cavalry were in touch with them. On the 11th we made a short march only, and halted for the night at La Belle Hôtesse. (See map 2.)

The morning of the 12th was foggy. We were leading regiment of the brigade, "A" Squadron forming the advanced guard. We marched via Wallon Cappel, Longue Croix, Sylvestre-Cappel to Eecke. The 3rd Cavalry Brigade on our right had meanwhile reconnoitred the Mont des Cats and found it held. They accordingly attacked it from the south, supported by their R.H.A. The Greys and "C" Squadron of ours started a frontal dismounted attack from the west. This hardly seemed a cavalry manœuvre. I should have thought that the fifty odd Huns on the hill could have been scuppered much more quickly by turning the position from both flanks. Anyway, the attack by the 5th Brigade was discontinued, and the 3rd Brigade captured the hill all right. We went into billets near Godewaersvelde.

We were now among people who talked nothing but Flemish, and we consequently found it very difficult to make ourselves understood. "Doo lay," etc., meant nothing to these people. But we found beer in place of vin blanc. On the 13th we advanced as far as Boeschoepe and Berthen, and had some scrapping with German patrols. "B" Squadron took two prisoners. In the evening we retired to billets at

Abeele Station. This is on the Belgian frontier. The station master was very friendly, but would insist on headquarter officers drinking some very sweet champagne he had got. On the 14th we marched to Kemmel, where we got in touch with the 3rd Cavalry Division, who had landed at Ostend with the 7th Division. We billeted at Kemmel, expecting a great cavalry action the next day.

We marched at 5.15 a.m. on the 15th, the brigade rendezvous being at Wytschaete. Lieuts. Thompson and Sparrow took patrols to reconnoitre the crossings over the Lys at Comines and Wervicq. They returned and reported that the bridge at Comines had been destroyed, but the one at Wervicq was intact. Lieut. Sparrow had an exciting encounter with some Germans, and was at one time in danger of being cut off. He finally evaded the enemy by jumping a wire fence with his whole patrol. The brigade advanced to Oosttaverne. From here the regiment was directed on Comines, "C" Squadron guarding the left flank by occupying Hollebeke and Houthem. They had to fight for both these places, Lieut. Thompson's troop capturing the former, Lieut. Goodhart's the latter. "A" and "B" Squadrons then advanced, dismounted on the left and right respectively of the Kortekeer Beck.

The enemy, who were in no great strength, fell back before us, and our two squadrons reached the line of the Comines-Warneton railway.

Soon after 2 p.m. we were ordered back from this position, so we retired on the horses which were about Garde Dieu, and finally marched back to billets at Kemmel. On the 16th we advanced once more to Oosttaverne, where we remained all day, being in brigade reserve.

As far as I remember, most of the officers foregathered in the estaminet, where they drank coffee and played "shove ha'penny." I think Major Richardson was a good winner. The Greys were meanwhile watching towards Comines and Houthem, and the 12th were at Garde Dieu. We finally went into billets near Oosttaverne. On the 17th we did not move till the afternoon. The regiment was then detailed to hold an outpost line from the Halte, a quarter-mile north of Houthem, to a point on the Hollebeke-Zandvoorde road. This gave us a front of about one and a quarter miles. " B " Squadron occupied a farm with troops in some trenches that existed already, " C " were in support, " A " and headquarters were in billets a bit north-west of Houthem. A lady of exceptional beauty was reported in the " B " Squadron farm. The O.C. wisely kept his young officers in the trenches all night !

Early on the 18th, " A " Squadron relieved " B " in the trenches. It had been a quiet night, but very cold. At 2.30 p.m. we were ordered to capture and hold Tenbrielen. " C " Squadron were ordered to turn the town from the left or north, and " B " from the right or south, " A " being in support. The two leading squadrons achieved their object, and cleared German snipers out of their respective portions of the town. We then sent the horses back to Houthem and put Tenbrielen in a state of defence. We remained there during the night without being molested, and were relieved by the Greys on the morning of the 19th.

From Tenbrielen we pushed on to America. Here our rôle was to protect the right flank of the 7th Division, who were to advance on Menin. We remained at America all day, being intermittently shelled, and at night were ordered back to billets at Kortewilde.

On the 20th we again moved forward to America on the same job as on the 19th. There was great activity on this day. Towards Wervicq our patrols were in touch with the enemy, and there was considerable shelling on both sides. At about 2 p.m. we were suddenly ordered back to Oosttaverne to support the 4th Cavalry Brigade, who were being attacked from the direction of Warneton.

As we left America, a frontal attack was developing against the 7th Division. We got back to Oosttaverne as quickly as we could. " C " Squadron were sent forward on the right of the Oosttaverne-Warneton road to hold a position covering the left of the 4th Cavalry Brigade. As they got into position, our own guns mistook them for Germans and shelled them pretty heavily. Capt. Barne, Lieut. Hatton, Sergt. Killick, Sergt. Goodwin, Corpl. Finley and another man were wounded. The enemy did not press his attack, and at about 5 p.m. orders were received to occupy a defensive position east of the Oosttaverne-Warneton road. The Greys were on the right of the brigade, and held ground astride this road, their right being in touch with the left of the 4th Cavalry Brigade. Our line faced south and east. In the salient was a farm among some trees that became known as "Edwards' Farm." The 12th Lancers were on our left. "C" Squadron were sorted out from the position they had got into on the right of the Greys, and rejoined the regiment. We were ordered to dig in. Alas! the entrenching tools had been jettisoned for the pursuit over the Marne. Lieut. Hall describes his experiences as follows:—

"Spent most of the night digging a trench with the aid of a broken plate, mess tins and knives and forks." Bayonets were also used, and a few spades were collected at Oosttaverne. The inhabitants, before parting with these, were insistent in demanding that they should be returned when we had finished with them! Poor devils! this was their first taste of war. They knew more about it a fortnight later, I expect. The sappers from the Field Troop did what they could for us, and their help was invaluable. We dug all night. On the right were "B" Squadron scratching in a ploughed field, and along the southern edge of "Edwards' Farm." The M.G. had, I think, taken up a position in the roof of the farm. "A" were on the left, chiefly holding the eastern edge of the farm grounds, "C" were in support at the farm. We failed to get touch with the 12th all night.

Early on the morning of the 21st, we had a look at our position by daylight. It was as bad a one as could well be imagined. The right, in the ploughed field, was on the forward face of a regular glacis sloping down to a small brook. The Huns could be seen digging like beavers on the top of the opposite ridge eight hundred yards away. "Edwards' Farm" was merely a dangerous salient. It possessed no field of fire at all, but would be sure to act as a magnet for every German shell that might come along. We began to look about for a second position. Immediately behind the farm we saw a ridge that seemed rather a good position. Certainly from this ridge it would be possible to bring heavy fire to bear on any enemy who might occupy the farm and try to debouch from it. We decided to get to work with our knives and forks

Chapter IV.

and put this ridge " in a state of defence." When we got there we found it already occupied by the right squadron of the 12th Lancers. In fact, our centre and left had spent the night immediately in front of their line ! We arranged matters with the 12th, who drew in a bit to their left, and the ridge became our second line of defence. We spent the morning improving our position. About noon the 3rd Cavalry Brigade, on the left of ours, retired a short way, the 12th Lancers conformed, and we had to conform to the 12th. While this retirement was in progress an order came from the Brigadier that we were to re-occupy our original positions. We accordingly advanced again. The Huns had, however, occupied " Edwards' Farm," and we finally had to dig in just behind the crest of the hill that was to have been our second position. Our line included a couple of cottages, with a small farm behind the centre for R.H.Q. Our left was in touch with the 12th at a convent they were holding, and our right was in touch with the Greys. The position was in fact a very much better one to hold than our first one had been.

The salient had been flattened out, we were behind the crest, and therefore not a good target for artillery, and yet we had quite a sufficient field of fire. On the right " C " Squadron had a very good field of fire over the ploughed field right down to the brook. I think " A " and " B " Squadrons each had one advanced trench on the crest of the hill for purposes of observation. In this position we dug some really good trenches, but we were new to the job. The idea that cavalry would have to dig themselves in had not, I think, occurred to many people before. The Colonel had a dug-out constructed about ten yards behind the trench line as an advanced headquarters. The architect of this structure was Lieut. Wyborn, who was attached to headquarters in charge of the cyclists. I well remember the first day the Brigadier came to see us, how the Brigade-Major, Captain Howard-Vyse, laughed at this dug-out because of its resemblance to the pictures in the Engineering Manual. Why this should cause laughter, I do not know, but it shows the spirit in which most cavalrymen regarded trenches at that time. Our horses were meanwhile behind Oosttaverne, with one officer, I think Lieut. Thompson, in charge. On the 22nd, a company of Indian troops relieved the Greys, who went into support for twenty-four hours. That night there was a lot of firing. Against the left of our line there was a Boche reconnaissance of some sort, which was repulsed by " A " Squadron. On the right, I don't think there was any attack at all. The Indians were rather fond of starting bursts of rapid fire either at imaginary enemies or, presumably, to make sure the bolts of their rifles were working properly. This firing spread to a portion of the right of our line. In the centre the enemy consisted chiefly of cows! Anyway, in the morning there were half-a-dozen lying dead about fifty yards in front of us.

The 23rd was a quiet day, except for a good bit of shelling The headquarters farm was hit and burnt down. A fresh farm was found for them a little farther back, and well down the reverse slope of the hill. This was a better place for rear headquarters, as it was on a road leading to Brigade Headquarters and also to the headquarters of the Greys and 12th. The Colonel still had his dug-out just behind the line as advanced headquarters.

The 24th passed quietly, the 12th being relieved for twenty-four hours by Indians and going into billets north of Oosttaverne. On the evening of the 25th it was our turn to be relieved. Indian troops took over our sector, and we went to Oosttaverne.

About 2 p.m. on the 26th we turned out, mounted, and formed up in readiness to support an attack which was being carried out by some Indian troops in the direction of Houthem. The attack was unable to make much headway, and we were not employed.

On the morning of the 27th, we again took over our original trenches. It was noticed that the enemy's activity was increasing. In particular, there was a lot of sniping going on. On the 28th there was more shelling by the enemy than there had ever been before, and his trenches seemed to have increased in number; there was also considerable rifle fire and activity by the patrols at night. A patrol of " A " Squadron picked up a dead Jaeger officer in front of their lines. During the 29th heavy firing could be heard away to the left, but on our front it was a quiet day. That evening the Greys were relieved by a company of Indians. All through the night wheeled trans-

Chapter IV.

port could be heard behind the German lines, presumably on the Houthem-Garde Dieu road. This was still going on the following morning. The information we received from higher authority had been so optimistic that we took this to indicate that the enemy were preparing to retire. It will be noticed that at first the regiment had been disposed with every man in the front line. We had no one at all in support. The last few days, however, the C.O. had made it a practice to withdraw two troops each day, soon after daybreak, as far as the headquarters farm, which was a very comfortable one, and to let them rest there for the day. On the 30th, two troops of " B " Squadron were resting.

Very soon the enemy began what for those days was a heavy bombardment all along our line; there was also a lot of sniping; and parties of Germans began to advance from the trenches where these were farthest from us. The troops who were resting were ordered up to the trenches. During the morning Lieut. Carew was killed by a sniper. All this time we could hear heavy fighting away to our left. At 2.15 p.m. a message was received that the 12th had been obliged to retire to conform with the troops on their left, and that they were evacuating the Convent. This was very serious for us, as if the enemy occupied the Convent they would enfilade all the left and centre of our line. The Colonel accordingly got out orders to withdraw in conformity with the 12th.

These were, however, quickly countermanded on receipt of a message that the 12th had re-occupied the Convent. At 3.15 p.m. we were again informed by the 12th that they had had to retire.

A verbal message then reached our left to the effect that once more they were going to re-occupy their line. This message was incorrect, as was realised when at 3.30 p.m. the Huns opened fire on us from the Convent. We were then forced to retire, and to retire quickly, too, to avoid being cut off. The retirement was covered by the 4th Troop of " B " Squadron, commanded by Sergeant Bassinthwaite, since Lieut. Carew had been killed that morning.

This Troop caused just sufficient delay to the enemy to enable the rest of the Regiment to get away. They were then overwhelmed and all, except one man, were killed or taken prisoners. The Regiment had to retire towards Oosttaverne till they could once more get in touch with the right of the 12th. The ground was very open, but the enemy, having reached our trenches, did not push on at all boldly. This was largely due to the fact that the retirement was very gallantly covered by the Machine Gun Section, under Lieut. McConnel, who came into action in the open, and had a very steadying effect on the Huns. We finally took up a position in front of Oosttaverne with a good field of fire but no trenches. Our left was in touch with the 12th, but our right, which rested on the Oosttaverne-Warneton road, was rather in the air, as the Indians, to whom we had passed word that we were retiring, had suffered considerable casualties and had got rather too far to the right. Eventually the Brigadier ordered a retirement to a position that had been chosen, and partly dug, about three-quarters of a mile north-west of Oosttaverne. As we were retiring to this position, Lieut. Micholls was wounded. He was badly hit in the abdomen and proved a very heavy weight to get along on a stretcher. He was most cheery about it, however, and owned that he had been hit in his biggest part! We got back to our new line without further trouble. The front had been considerably shortened, and the Indians were withdrawn temporarily. Our right was in touch with the 4th Cavalry Brigade and our left with the 12th Lancers. The Greys were in Brigade Reserve. Our casualties on this day had been: Lieut. Carew and three men killed; Lieut. Micholls and eight men wounded; seventeen men were missing (the 4th Troop of "B").

The night was spent digging in. We had got some picks and shovels now, and by the morning had made some quite good trenches.

During the 31st there was considerable shelling away to our right, about Messines, and on our left, between St. Eloi and Ypres. Along our front things were pretty quiet. We were disposed with "B" Squadron on the right, "A" in the centre, and "C" on the left. In the evening the Greys relieved the 12th, who went into reserve. French troops also began to arrive with a view to taking over from us, and, I think, of attacking. A French regiment of infantry was at

St. Eloi, and sent one company to support us. This company was disposed as though we were not there at all. They threw out a line of scouts to the front, and these proceeded to dig themselves in about one hundred yards in advance of " A " Squadron.

The remainder were disposed behind hedges in the centre of our position. The Company Commander shared the one cottage in the place with our Regimental Headquarters. In front of the right of our position there was a small wood, " B " Squadron being thrown back so as to be able to fire at one edge of it, and " A " Squadron having one troop (the 4th, under Lieut. Silvertop) facing almost to their right so as to fire into another edge of it. At about 11 p.m. a heavy attack was made on the 4th Cavalry Brigade. This they repulsed. At about 1 a.m. (1st November) the Germans made another attack on the same part of the line. Their troops, in advancing to this attack, marched in column of route through the wood on our right, and Lieut. Silvertop's troop claim to have done considerable execution, as they opened rapid fire at about three hundred yards. Eventually the Germans drove in the left of the 4th Cavalry Brigade and occupied their trenches. From this position they could enfilade the position held by " B " Squadron. Captain Little therefore withdrew a short distance. Regimental H.Q. and " A " Squadron in the centre were able to hold the salient thus created, but our line had been considerably lengthened.

The gap between Headquarters and " B " was accordingly filled by some of the French troops.

The Germans in their attack had occupied not only the trenches held by the 4th Brigade, and, I think, by some Indian troops, but also the village of Wytschaete. They had here got themselves into rather a dangerous salient, for the 1st Cavalry Division still held the Messines Ridge south of Wystchaete, and we were holding ground under a mile north-east of that village.

General Chetwode ordered the 12th to counter-attack Wystchaete at dawn. Captain Little and " B " Squadron threw in their lot with the 12th, the French taking over the front occupied by " B." The counter-attack was completely successful. The Boche appeared thoroughly disorganised and put up very little resistance. The village was cleared and the trenches orginally held by the Household Regiment of the 4th Brigade were reached. " B " Squadron took a particular delight in avenging the fate of their 4th Troop. Captain Little shot a Hun with his revolver, which caused his friends who had observed him on the range to remark that that Hun was a very unlucky man. In this opinion, I think, the O.C. " B " himself concurred. It was during this attack that Sergeant Gray (3rd Troop) spotted a Boche looking out of a windmill. Ned Gray had always been a crack shot, as well as being famous for a fine supply of expletives. With a shout of " there's a beggar " (or words to that effect) he up with his rifle and dropped the Hun neatly out of the window. The enemy started shelling the trenches that had been retaken, and the 12th and " B " Squadron were ordered to retire.

They handed over the village of Wytschaete to the French. During the morning our Allies also relieved the rest of our Brigade, in fact, the whole of the 2nd Cavalry Division. As we were being withdrawn the enemy began a bombardment with what became known as " Black Marias " or " Jack Johnsons." The French Company Commander had not been informed that we were to be withdrawn so soon, although he had already taken over the whole line. To him it appeared a bad moment to choose for a retirement, and for a minute or two the " entente " seemed in danger. Lieut. McConnel, who with the machine guns was the last to leave, saved the situation by staying behind with the French till the " straffe " was over and the position had been explained. For his action on this day and in covering the retirement on the 30th, he deservedly got a D.S.O., as did also Captain Little over the Wytschaete affair. Our casualties this day were not heavy, but among them was Lieut. Silvertop, who was wounded during the withdrawal.

The horses had been moved back on the 30th October, and we now rejoined them at Voormezeele. We then marched via Kemmel and La Clytte to billets at Mille Kruis. Here we re-organised as best we could. A Signalling Officer was dispensed with, the present writer going to " A " Squadron as Second in Command, vice Lieut. Micholls.

Chapter IV.

On the 2nd November we marched to Lindenhoek, just east of Kemmel Hill, where we remained in support most of the day. In the afternoon we were withdrawn, and went right back to billets at La Manche, about one mile south-west of Mont Noir. On the 3rd we moved up to Dranoutre, where we remained till the afternoon. In the evening we moved on to Neuve Eglise, where we left our horses and marched to trenches just north-east of Wulverghem. We took these over from, I think, some of the 1st Cavalry Brigade. We spent a quiet night. On the morning of the 4th we were relieved in a thick fog by the 3rd Cavalry Brigade, and marched back to Neuve Eglise. We rejoined our horses and spent the day just behind Neuve Eglise, going into billets close by for the night.

We stood to on the morning of the 5th till about 11 a.m., and then retired to La Manche, where we went into billets. There we stayed all the 6th, indulging in a football match that afternoon. "B" Squadron beat "A" 1—0. We left billets about 3 p.m. on the 7th and marched to Wulverghem. From here the horses were sent back to Dranoutre, where they joined "B" echelon. The regiment held barricades in Wulverghem for the night. We were very much mixed up with the French at this time. They were immediately on our right, and they held trenches in front of us; in fact, we were supporting them, and they were barricading the roads behind us.

"B" echelon shared a farm with a regiment of French cavalry.

We stayed about Wulverghem all the 8th, and marched back to the horses on the morning of the 9th. We then went into very comfortable billets at La Creche, one mile north of Steenwerke. Here we remained all the 10th. On that day some remounts joined and were very welcome, as the horses had had rather a bad time and a good many had gone sick. The quality of the remounts was, however, poor.

The next day we moved up to Wulverghem and took over some trenches there in the evening. our right being in touch with the French. We remained there till the evening of the 13th, when we were relieved by the 16th Lancers. We had a very quiet time, but it had been alternately very wet and very cold. In fact, we were coming to the conclusion that November was not the right time of the year to be at war at all. Those of us with a Classical education remembered how much better Julius Cæsar had managed affairs "in hibernis castris."

We returned to our billets at La Creche and stayed there till the 15th. During the afternoon of that day we moved to billets west of Neuve Eglise. Here we were in support to troops in the trenches. We never got any further, however, and returned to La Creche on the 17th. The weather had turned very cold by now and there had been some snow. On the 18th we had a false alarm and turned out and saddled up, but nothing happened. On the 19th we moved up to trenches one mile north of Kemmel. It was a horrible evening, combining wind, rain, snow and frost. We left our horses in the snow, and they were taken back to billets by the horseholders. We then marched to the trenches on foot and took over from some French Chasseurs Alpins. "A" and "C" Squadrons were in the front line and "B" in support. The support trench was only about 150 yards behind the front line. These trenches were our first experience of trenches in close proximity to the Huns. In places they were only 75 yards away. The Frenchmen were astounded at the number of officers we had in proportion to men. In the light of later events, we certainly had too many, as we only left one officer in charge of all the horses. As an instance, "A" Squadron, with one major, one captain, and two or three subalterns, took over a trench line, the garrison of which had been commanded by a French sergeant. The latter was quite worried about it, and could not think that any of his trenches would be "très chic pour un Commandant."

It is interesting to notice that although these trenches were so close to the Germans, there were no communication trenches. We just walked straight into the front line over the top, and this on a frosty night with snow on the ground that crackled violently under our feet. Yet the relief took place without our being in any way disturbed by the enemy. These trenches, which had been made by the French, were provided with "overhead cover." All firing was done through loopholes. There was very little wire, and I should think the

Chapter IV.

position would easily have been rushed by a surprise assault.

It would have been impossible from such trenches to bring good rapid fire to bear.

We remained in the trenches all the 22nd, a lovely bright frosty day. There was a good bit of sniping on both sides, and the Huns shelled us at times with "Black Marias." Our guns seemed to be very quiet, and this although parties of Germans could be observed nearly all day at work about half a mile behind the lines. The regiment had about half-a-dozen casualties, and were relieved during the night of the 21st by the 5th Dragoon Guards. Our horses had been brought to meet us, and we rode back to billets near Steenwerk, getting there at about 1 a.m. on the 22nd. There was a hard frost and the roads were very slippery, being covered in places by a sheet of ice.

This was our last experience of what may, I suppose, be termed the First Battle of Ypres, for we were not employed again for some weeks.

Our billets at Steenwerk were good as billets went in those days, and we remained in them until the 15th of January, 1915.

From the above account it will be seen that the regiment came in for very little heavy fighting during the First Battle of Ypres.

I will explain briefly the rôle we were filling. At the beginning of the battle the 1st and 2nd Cavalry Divisions were covering the advance of the 2nd and 3rd Corps into Flanders. In so doing we encountered German cavalry who were protecting the right of the German line. As that line extended northwards, this cavalry also covered the front of the German right.

We slowly pushed the German cavalry back till they were relieved by infantry and jaegers. By then our infantry were in close touch with the enemy east of Ypres and about Armentières.

The 1st and 2nd Cavalry Divisions then had to fill the gap between these places. It was in doing this that we had to fight as infantry pure and simple. We came in for the heavy German attacks on 30th October and 1st November, but even on these days the attacks were not so heavy on our front as they were on the 1st Corps front at Ypres and on the 1st Cavalry Division at Messines. After being definitely withdrawn from the line on the 22nd November, we at once set about re-organising, replacing casualties, and learning infantry work. Bayonet exercises became a great feature in our training. When "B" Squadron got to work with their bayonets at Wytschaete they did great execution, but their methods were probably of a rough-and-ready order. I don't suppose they stopped at the "two inches" of steel that Colonel Campbell afterwards recommended for a Hun's kidneys. At least one man I know made quite sure of his Boche each time by first sticking him and then letting off a round before withdrawing his bayonet.

Attention was also paid to physical training; runs, tugs-of-war, and football were indulged in to keep the men fit.

On the 2nd December we were inspected by His Majesty the King, and on the 7th by the Commander-in-Chief. Short leave had started, which at first was confined to seventy-two hours in England.

In this way we settled down into winter quarters.

CHAPTER V—1915 & 1916.

(*See Maps I, II & III*)

ON the 15th January we were withdrawn two days' march further west to Fauquembergues and Renty (Map I.).
Here we had very comfortable billets indeed. "A" Squadron were at Renty; Brigade Headquarters, Regimental Headquarters, and "B" and "C" Squadrons were in Fauquembergues. We stayed here till 3rd of February, when we again set out eastwards, as we were to take over trenches in the Ypres sector. The plan was that the Cavalry Corps should relieve some French troops who were temporarily withdrawn into reserve. We were thus to fight in the French Northern Army, at that time commanded by General Foch. We were to be supported by French artillery. The 2nd Cavalry Division formed two dismounted brigades. "A" Brigade, consisting of the 4th Cavalry Brigade, 4th Hussars, and two Squadrons 5th Lancers, under General Bingham; "B" Brigade, consisting of the 5th Cavalry Brigade, 16th Lancers, and one Squadron 5th Lancers, under General Chetwode.

(See Map II). On the 3rd February we marched from Fauquembergues, stopped that night near St. Venant, and got to billets at Verte Rue, north of Merville, on the 4th February. We stayed there till the 13th, and employed our time doing intensive training in infantry work, including the making of bombs by filling jam tins with explosives, nails, stones, etc. We also studied the art of throwing these very elementary weapons of war. They did not always detonate quite as they should have done. On 13th February we set out by motor-'bus for Ypres. I will try and give a list of the officers who accompanied the party :—

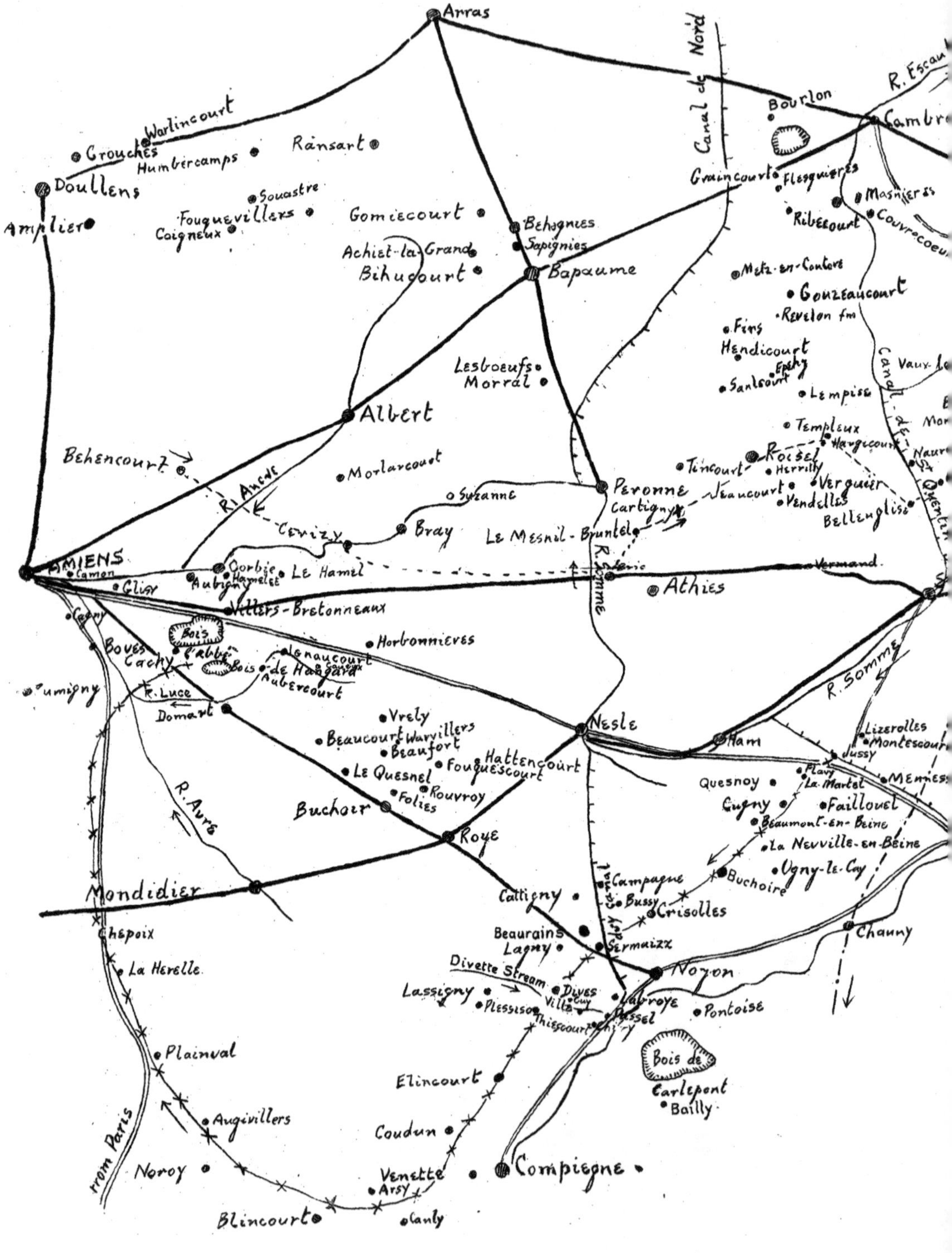
Arras
Canal du Nord
Bourlon
R. Escaut
Cambrai
Warlincourt
Grouches
Humbercamps
Ransart
Doullens
Souastre
Fouquevillers
Coigneux
Amplier
Gomiecourt
Behagnies
Sapignies
Achiet-la-Grand
Bihucourt
Bapaume
Graincourt
Flesquières
Masnières
Ribecourt
Metz-en-Couture
Gouzeaucourt
Revelon fm
Fins
Heudicourt
Epehy
Sorel
Lempire
Lesboeufs
Morval
Albert
Templeux
Hargicourt
Behencourt
Morlancourt
R. Ancre
Tincourt
Roisel
Hervilly
Suzanne
Peronne
Jeancourt
Verguier
Vendelles
Cartigny
Bellenglise
Cerizy
Bray
Le Mesnil-Bruntel
R. Somme
Vermand
AMIENS
Camon
Glisy
Corbie
Aubigny
Hamelet
Le Hamel
Athies
Villers-Bretonneaux
Cagny
Horbonnières
Boves
Bois l'abbé
Cachy
Ignaucourt
Bois de Hangard
Aubercourt
Dury
R. Luce
Domart
Vrely
Beaucourt
Warvillers
Beaufort
Hattencourt
Fouquescourt
Le Quesnel
Rouvroy
Folies
Buchoir
Roye
R. Avre
Nesle
Ham
R. Somme
Lizerolles
Montescourt
Jussy
Flavy
Quesnoy
Cugny
Menessis
Faillouel
Beaumont-en-Beine
La Neuville-en-Beine
Ugny-le-Gay
Buchoire
Mondidier
Campagne
Bussy
Crisolles
Chauny
Canal
Beaurains
Lagny
Sermaize
Divette Stream
Dives
Noyon
Lassigny
Ville
Plessis
Larbroye
Passel
Pontoise
Thiescourt
Chepoix
La Herelle
Plainval
Bois de Carlepont
Bailly
Elincourt
Augivillers
Coudun
from Paris
Noroy
Venette
Compiegne
Arsy
Blincourt
Canly

AP III.

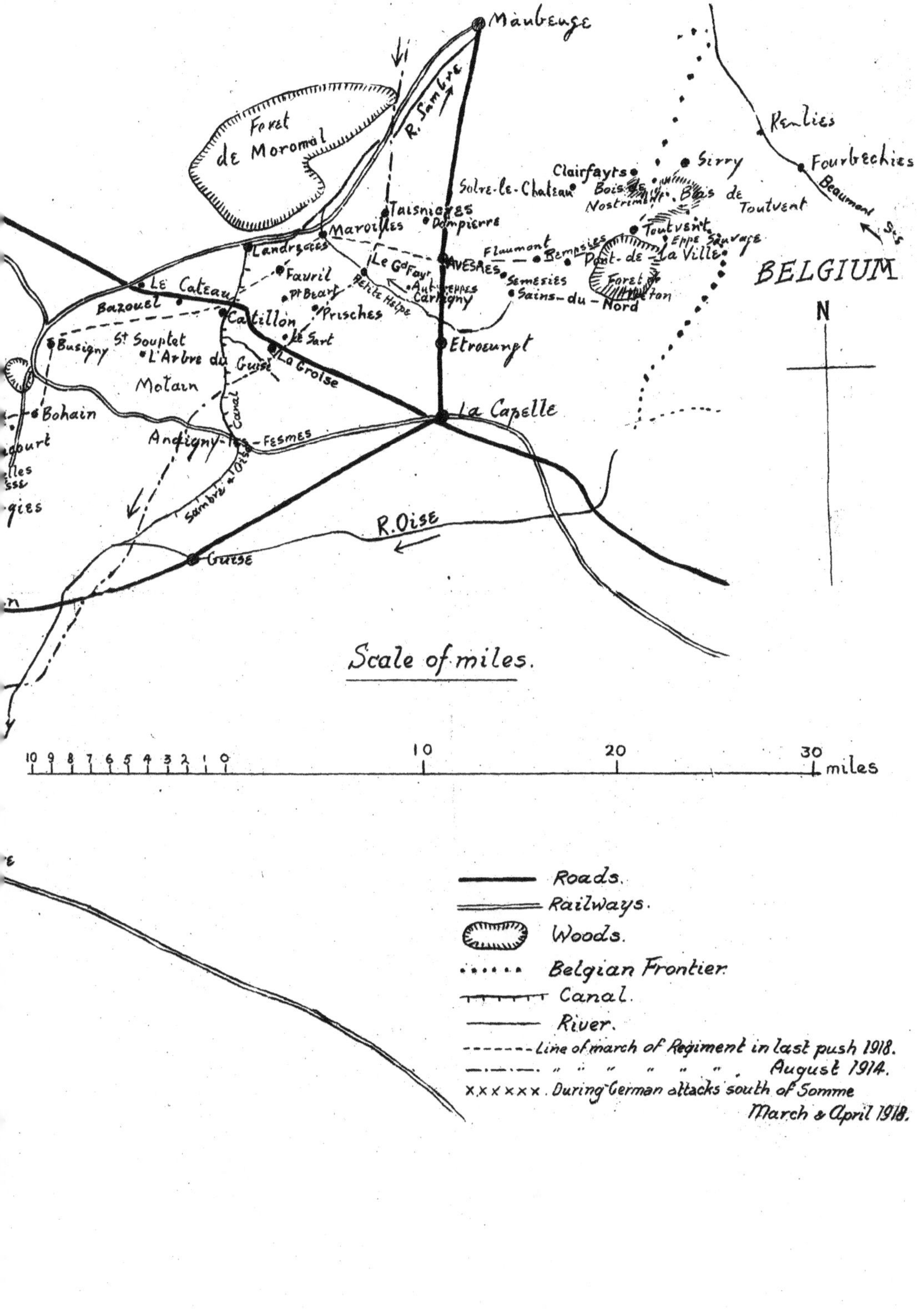

Maubeuge
Foret de Moromal
R. Sambre
Renlies
Fourbechies
Beaumont
Sirry
Clairfayts
Bois de Toutvent
Solre-le-Chateau
Taisnieres
Dompierre
Maroilles
Toutvent
Eppe Sauvage
Flaumont
Landrecies
Le Gd Fayt
AVESNES
Pont-de-la Ville
BELGIUM
N
Le Cateau
Fauril
Petite Helpe
Semesies
Sains-du-Nord
Bazouel
Pt Beart
Prisches
Catillon
Le Sart
Busigny
St Souplet
L'Arbre du Guise
La Groise
Etroeungt
Motain
Canal
Bohain
La Capelle
Andigny-les-Fesmes
Sambre & Oise
R. Oise
Guise
Scale of miles.
10 9 8 7 6 5 4 3 2 1 0
10
20
30 miles
Roads.
Railways.
Woods.
Belgian Frontier.
Canal.
River.
Line of march of Regiment in last push 1918.
" " " " " " August 1914.
x x x x x x . During German attacks south of Somme March & April 1918.

1915 & 1916

Headquarters.
Lieut.-Col. Edwards, C.B.
Major, Cook.
Capt. & Adjt. Sanford.
Lieut. McConnel, D.S.O.
Lieut. Adams.

" A " Squadron.	*" B " Squadron.*	*" C " Squadron.*
Major Richardson.	Capt. Darling.	Capt. Mangles.
Capt. Wybrants (late of 14th Hussars).	Lieut. Hall.	Lieut. Sparrow.
Lieut. Dodgson.	Lieut. Barr (late 3rd Hussars).	Lieut. Thompson.
Lieut. Wyborn.	Lieut. Whidborne (14th Hussars).	Lieut. Goodhart.
Lieut. Burke.		

Capt. Little was sick in England, having broken his collarbone hunting while home on leave.

R.S.M. Austin was with Headquarters, as was Sergeant Beavon (Signalling Sergeant). The three S.S.M.'s were Nash (" A "), Reader (" B "), and Smith (" C "). The S.Q.M.S.'s were the same as on mobilisation.

Our fleet of motor-'buses deposited us in the middle of the night in the Square at Ypres. We then went into various houses and cellars round the Convent, as our Brigade was in reserve. " A " Brigade was in the trenches east of Zillebeke. At that time Ypres had been shelled to a certain extent, but a lot of the houses were quite sound. The town was still full of civilians, some of whom continued to do a brisk trade in Belgian lace. The men were exercised in small parties under an officer, and if a Hun aeroplane was seen, everyone took cover. It was hoped in this way to conceal from the enemy the fact that there were any troops in the town. Certainly the Boche was very kind to us and shelled the place very little.

The 27th and 28th Divisions, who had not been in France very long, were holding trenches immediately on the right of our Division, and were having a good lot of fighting, losing trenches and then counter-attacking to get them back. While we were in Ypres we were continually being warned to be in readiness to support these Divisions. We were, however, not actually needed. On the evening of the 18th February our Brigade relieved " A " Brigade in the trenches. The Regiment took over from the Oxford Yeomanry. " A " Squadron were on the right, in touch with the Greys, and " B " on the left, in touch with the 12th. " C " Squadron

Chapter V.

were in Brigade Reserve in some rudimentary sort of dug-outs.

The trenches were really breastworks, and were in a wood east of Zillebeke. The German trenches were from forty to a hundred yards away. The intervening space was covered with a mass of fallen trees, and would have been very difficult to attack over. Being in a wood, neither side could shell the front line of the other, consequently the sector was of necessity a very quiet one.

The trenches, such as they were, were dry and were well provided with trench-boards; in fact, they were the best we had seen up to date.

Regimental Headquarters were in a sort of hut or shanty that had been constructed by the French at the rear edge of the wood. It had a little earth thrown over it and a few sods, but was in no way shell-proof. As a protection from bombs, it was covered with wire netting. I think it was the O.C. " C " Squadron who was feeling funny one morning and asked Sergt.-Major Lee whether he kept birds in this cage. His answer was brief and characteristic: " No, sir. Rabbits."

We tried to liven things up with a little sniping, but did not often get a target. One morning, in broad daylight, Sergeants Gray and Curran, of " B " Squadron, did a raid on their own, got behind the German lines, and shot a Boche. " Paddy " Curran then began to " see red," so Ned Gray got him back to our lines as best he could. The Boche retaliated with a bit of sniping, but inflicted no casualties.

Experiments were made with elementary trench mortars, but these were not a great success, and had a habit of falling short, so the Squadron Leaders in the front line politely (?) requested that the experiments should be discontinued.

Things were very quiet till the morning of 21st February. At about 6.30 a.m. that day the Germans managed to blow up a trench of the 16th Lancers, who were on the left of the 12th. This was done either by mining or by laying a charge against the parapet. The Germans then rushed the trench and occupied it. The 16th had heavy casualties, including ten officers. There is no doubt that at that time the cavalry took far too many officers to the trenches. " C " Squadron, of ours, were immediately sent up and placed under the orders of Colonel Eccles, commanding the 16th, with a view to counter-attacking. About one company of French infantry, who were in support, also came up. Before employing the French troops, reference had, however, to be made to higher authority. This wasted a lot of valuable time, and it was 10 a.m. before the counter-attack started. By this time the Huns had got thoroughly settled in the captured trench, and the attacking forces came under a heavy fire as soon as they advanced. They got to within fifty yards or so of the position, and then the attack stopped dead, the French having lost heavily, including the Company Commander, who was killed. In " C " Squadron seven men had been killed, and Captain Mangles, Lieut. Sparrow, Lieut. Goodhart, and three men wounded. Lieut. Thompson was thus the only officer left. In the position that had been reached the troops found a certain amount of cover, and there they had to remain until after dark, when they were withdrawn. Meanwhile a new trench had been dug in rear of the former one, and a plan was being devised for bombing or mining the Huns out of what they had captured.

Sergeant Simes, " C " Squadron, was awarded the D.C.M. for coolness and gallantry during the attack and in getting back some of the wounded.

On the 22nd, Lieut. McConnel made an attempt to blow in a German sap that ran close up to " A " Squadron's trenches. He managed to drop some charges of gun cotton into the sap and to detonate them. It was never discovered what damage had been done.

On the morning of the 23rd, Lieut. Barr was killed by a German sniper. That night we were relieved by some of the 1st Cavalry Brigade. The whole 2nd Cavalry Division was withdrawn, and we returned to Verte Rue by 'bus. On the 27th the Regiment went back to Renty and Fauquembergues. Here Captain Barne rejoined from England, having recovered from his wound, and took over command of " C " Squadron. We stayed at Fauquembergues till the 9th of March, when we once more moved up to Verte Rue, this time to take part in the 1st Army attack at Neuve Chapelle. This was, I think, the first big attack that the British Army had made since trench warfare began. Before the attack took place the enemy held Neuve Chapelle. Sir Douglas Haig's intention was to capture that village and the Aubers Ridge,

Chapter V.

and then to push some cavalry through the gap to exploit the success. On the 10th of March, after what for those days was a very heavy bombardment, the attack began. At first it was a great success, the village of Neuve Chappelle was quickly captured, as was the German front line trench on a frontage of three thousand five hundred yards. Our Brigade was moved up to Rouge Croix, a mile and a half north-west of Neuve Chappelle. Here we awaited events. Quite an imposing lot of German prisoners came by, being marched to the rear, but there were also a large number of our own wounded in ambulances and on foot. We finally spent the night near Rouge Croix, horses in the open, most of the men in barns. The officers all shared one large room. It was on this night that Sergt.-Major Lee gave one of his all-too-rare hints on cookery, when he informed the Colonel that omelettes cannot be made without eggs. This was in answer to a complaint by the C.O. that one of the Squadrons had got an omelette, whereas Headquarters had none.

On the 11th we stood to all day, but were not employed, and billeted that night at La Gorgue, close to Estaires. On the 12th we remained at La Gorgue till 3 p.m., when we were moved up to Rouge Croix. From there we were sent on in some haste, to go through the infantry and take up the pursuit. Someone passed an order down to see that swords would draw easily. This went right down the Regiment and raised great hopes. As the Greys neared the front line they found that we had been sent up on an altogether too sanguine report. The Huns were not on the run, and our infantry were held up everywhere. We returned to La Gorgue, and the next day to Verte Rue. This first attempt to push cavalry through the " gap " had proved abortive. However, after this some such scheme formed a part, and indeed a leading feature, of every plan of attack.

We stayed at Verte Rue till the 23rd of April, the chief event being a very successful 2nd Cavalry Division Horse Show at Vieux Berguin on the 17th. On the 15th Major Little rejoined from England and went back to " B " Squadron. Captain Darling, from " B," took over command of " C " Squadron.

On the 18th, Major-General Kavanagh took over the

2nd Cavalry Division from General Gough, who went to the 7th Infantry Division. On the 23rd April, Squadrons were at exercise as usual when an order was suddenly received about 11 a.m. for the Brigade to assemble at La Courrone at 11.45 a.m. Cyclists were despatched to collect Squadrons and exercise parties, and in a creditably and incredibly short time the Regiment was on parade. This was the occasion of the Huns' historic and infamous attack with poison gas on some French Colonial troops who were holding trenches north of Ypres. We marched to Boeshepe, four miles south of Poperinghe, and finally back to Berthen, where we spent the night. On the 24th we marched viâ Reninghelst and Vlamertinghe, and spent the day north of that place. Lieuts. Whidborne, Conant and Hall, all of " B " Squadron, took out patrols either for local protection or to reconnoitre routes to different points in the line. In the evening we returned to Vlamertinghe. Here we left the horses with the horse-holders and spent the night in huts, being organised as a dismounted regiment. I think the horses went to Reninghelst. On the 26th, at 7 p.m., we marched through Ypres and along the railway and occupied reserve trenches south of Potijze. We got shelled a bit getting in, and S.S.M. Smith (" C " Squadron) was wounded. I have not got an accurate list of the officers who accompanied the regiment on this occasion, but I think the following is not far wrong :—

Headquarters.
    Lieut.-Col. Edwards, C.B.
    Major Cook, D.S.O.
    Capt. Sanford.
    Lieut. McConnel, D.S.O.
    Lieut. Adams.

" A " Squadron.	" B " Squadron.	" C " Squadron.
Major Richardson.	Major Little, D.S.O.	Capt. Darling.
Lieut. Dodgson.	Lieut. Hall.	Capt. Barne.
Lieut. Wyborn.	Lieut. Whidborne.	Lieut. F. Stout.
Lieut. Burke.	Lieut. Conant.	Lieut. Macintyre.
Lieut. Johns.		Lieut. Hatton.

We remained in the trenches till the 29th, sending working parties each night to the neighbourhood of Hooge. On the 29th we moved to other reserve trenches just north of Potijze. There was a lot more shelling here. One shell hit " B " Squadron headquarter dug-out and killed two or three

Chapter V.

men, including Corpl. Stanesby, a good footballer. In the afternoon of 2nd May, we were withdrawn altogether. Just as we were leaving, another gas attack began on the troops holding the north of the salient. The last squadron to go ("C") stuffed their handkerchiefs into their mouths, which was the only anti-gas measure we had devised at that time. The gas was chlorine. The attack failed as the wind changed, also there were some very stout fellows there to meet it, I think largely a battalion of Royal Dublin Fusiliers. We marched back ten miles to Ouderdom, some of the regiment getting shelled on the way. The next day we marched mounted to Ledringhem (north of Cassel), where we had very comfortable billets. The sight of the fresh country in the spring was very pleasant after the scene of desolation and destruction near Potijze cross-roads. This horrible spot was chiefly famous for heavy shelling and the stench of dead horses. It was remarkable that among all this a nightingale used to sing most delightfully every night, as though he quite liked war. While we were at Ledringhem we got our first respirators. These were made locally. They consisted of pads of material that were soaked in some chemical and stuffed into the mouth in case of gas.

We left Ledringhem on the 7th May and marched back to our old billets at Verte Rue. On the 9th of May the big Allied attack started at Arras. We "stood to" for two days in case there should be a gap for us to go through. No gap appeared, so we stood down again. On the 13th the Huns made another gas attack east of Ypres, and during the night 13th-14th, the 5th Cavalry Brigade was moved by motor 'bus to Vlamertinghe. About 10 p.m. on the 14th we took over front line trenches east of Potijze from the 3rd Cavalry Division. Some units of this division had made a brilliant counter-attack and had chased the Huns, in the words of the Essex Yeomanry, "clean out of our country." We took over from the 3rd Dragoon Guards. They had suffered heavy casualties, their Colonel was badly wounded, and I think they had only got two officers left. The trenches were badly damaged. The Boches were somewhere about 1,000 yards away. During the night we dug a new trench line about 150 yards in front of the old one. By the morning we had got quite good trenches. An infantry working party had helped us by constructing communication trenches leading back to the old trenches. All three squadrons were in the front line, " C " on the left in touch with the 12th Lancers, " B " in the centre, " A " on the right. The right of the line rested on the Ypres-Zonnebeke railway. South of the railway we joined up with the infantry; I think the 28th Division. We remained in these trenches till the 21st May. Patrols went out every night, but never really got in touch with the Germans. They were a long way off.

On our sector of the front there was very little shelling by either side. We had very few casualties, but these included Sergeant Tester killed and Sergeant "Paddy" Curran wounded. The night of the 21st we were relieved by infantry, and marched back to huts near Vlamertinghe. At about 3.30 a.m. on the 24th we suddenly got the order to turn out. The air was full of gas. There had evidently been another gas attack east of Ypres. This attack had fallen on the 1st Cavalry Division. The 9th Lancers and 18th Hussars, to name only two units, had had very heavy casualties.

The 2nd Cavalry Division relieved the 1st Cavalry Division that night. Our brigade was in divisional reserve, and occupied casements and dug-outs in the ramparts at Ypres. We stayed there four days sending out working parties each night to improve the trenches in the front line. The night of the 29th we were relieved by the Essex Yeomanry (3rd Cavalry Division), and returned by 'bus to Verte Rue, getting back there on Sunday morning, 30th May. The following day we marched to billets at Zuytpeene, just west of Cassel. These were very comfortable. Horses were in the open, but at this time of the year I think they did better there than in stuffy stables. We remained in this neighbourhood till the 5th of August. The British Army seemed to be acting all through this summer entirely on the defensive.

The enemy were also making no offensive on the western front. They were devoting their efforts to the east, where they were working their own sweet will, breaking up the much talked about "Russian steam roller." The only part we took in the war was to send working parties to such places as Dickebusch to construct second and third lines of defence,

Chapter V.

and strong points behind the front. Early in June, Lieut. Hall left us to go to the Royal Flying Corps as an observer. He remained with them for about three months, and then came back to the regiment as signalling officer. In July, Lieut. McConnel went as an instructor at a machine gun school, and was away from the regiment for the rest of the war. Lieut. F. Stout took over the Machine Gun Section. On 17th July, Brigadier-General Chetwode assumed command of 2nd Cavalry Division vice General Kavanagh, who, I think, got a corps. Lieut.-Colonel Wormald, 12th Lancers, got the 5th Brigade, Colonel Bulkely-Johnson, Greys, having already got command of the 8th Cavalry Brigade.

On 6th August we moved a few miles to Wittes (see Map 1), and Warne just north of Aire. Here again we were very comfortable. Soon after we got to these billets, polo was started in the brigade. It was appropriate that it should be in the billets of the 12th Lancers, the winners of the 1914 inter-regimental. The ground was too rough for a polo ball, so a small football was used.

It was while we were here that we conceived the idea of re-organising the horses of squadrons by colours. Nominally " A " had always been bay, " B " black and brown, and " C " chestnut. Actually, " B " and " C " had always had a good many bays. During the war, remounts had been posted to squadrons, regardless of colour. Great horse coping now took place, and in more than one case the tail scissors had to be resorted to in order to persuade the O.C. the other squadron to take what of course was really a very fine horse in exchange for one of his ! Some diversion was also caused by practising swimming the horses over the Aire Canal, in preparation for the grand pursuit after we should have gone through the mythical " gap."

In this pursuit we were to take the rivers and canals of Flanders, and even the Rhine itself it would seem, as it were in our stride.

We stayed in these billets until the 21st September, when we started moving south to take part in the Battle of Loos. A " gap " scheme for the cavalry had, of course, been included in the programme of this attack. It was even rumoured that the Franco-British attack near Loos and the

French attack in Champagne were to meet somewhere in the neighbourhood of Sedan, thus compassing the destruction of all the German forces in the salient. It was at any rate with some such optimistic view of the immediate future that we once more set out to have a look at the war. "B" Echelon was left behind, and we intended to be a real mobile force. On the 21st we marched to Estrée Blanche, where we stayed till the 24th. That day we moved to Equirre, and on the 25th to Cauchy à la Tour, where we arrived at 10.15 p.m. There had been great delay on the roads, as two columns moving up to the battle seemed to have crossed each other's line of march. It poured with rain all the afternoon and evening. This evening brought out the extraordinary character of the British soldier. When he is comfortable he grouses, when he is uncomfortable he is happy. This evening was as uncomfortable a march as could be imagined. At one point we were halted for fully an hour in a dingy mining village in the pouring rain. The men beguiled the time by bursting into song, and kept this up in the most cheerful manner the whole while. Pte. "Bob" Razzle, of "C" Squadron, delighted a large and admiring crowd with an exhibition of clog dancing. No wonder the British Army proved invincible to the Boche as well as to the weather. We remained in billets all the 26th. On the 27th we turned out at 4 a.m. and marched south. We suddenly halted and marched back again. I believe "someone had blundered." The brigade staff first read their orders to mean that we were to move to a certain place. On reading them a second time, on the line of march, they discovered that this was only to happen if something else happened first. The something else did not happen. We got back to billets just in time to see civilians disappearing with the last of the hay that we had had to leave behind. However, parties were quickly sent off to purchase more locally. I remember there was a little trouble about it later when the bills had to be paid. However, it all came right in the end. The horses got their hay, and the British taxpayer paid for it ungrudgingly. We stayed in billets all the 28th, ready to move if required. The weather had turned very wet and cold. On the 29th we were withdrawn to Nédonchelle. Here we were destined to remain for a bit. On the 2nd October, thirty men were sent under Captain Beech as a con-

Chapter V.

tribution to a divisional party who were to "clear the battlefield." Many volunteered for this (the signalling officer among them), expecting to get some souvenirs. Actually they were employed almost entirely in the unpleasant duty of burying the dead, a duty rendered doubly unpleasant by the fact that the dead were mostly British. Brigadier-General Wormald was commanding the party from the division, and on the 4th October he was killed by a shell. Colonel C. Campbell, 16th Lancers, succeeded him in command of the 5th Cavalry Brigade. Almost the same day, our C.O., Colonel Edwards, got command of an infantry brigade. Major Cook got the regiment, Major Richardson went to headquarters as second in command, and Captain Sanford took over " A " Squadron. Lieut. Hall became Adjutant vice Captain Sanford, and Lieut. MacIntyre, " C " Squadron, became Signalling Officer. Lieut. Goodhart rejoined from England, and went to " B " Squadron, and Lieut. Sturt joined and went to " C." Captain Micholls also rejoined, and went to " B " Squadron as second in command.

It was at this time that the question was raised of cavalry officers going to infantry battalions as C.O.'s and seconds in command. For the moment, no one went from the regiment. The cavalry were now withdrawn altogether, and on the 20th October we moved to Bourthes. We did not like these billets as winter quarters, and on the 24th October we moved to the neighbourhood of Moncavrel Here we were very comfortable, each squadron getting a large area comprising one or two small villages. All horses were under cover, and " C " Squadron officers had a " château " with a big bath, to the huge joy of Myles Thompson, who was now second in command of " C," Captain Barne having gone on the staff. On 9th November, Captain Sanford went home to take over second in command of an infantry battalion. Captain Micholls took over " A " Squadron.

On 16th November, owing to a re-arrangement of billets, we moved to Fauquemberges and Renty. Headquarters and " B " went to the former, " A " and " C " to the latter. On 30th November, Major Richardson went home to take command of the 26th Northumberland Fusiliers. We were now settled down in winter quarters, and really very comfortable.

During November we had had a digging party away constructing rear lines of defence, but during December the regiment was all in billets, and doing intensive infantry training in preparation for taking over a trench line early in the new year.

A fresh organisation had been worked out for the cavalry when called on to hold trenches as infantry. General Bingham was now commanding the Cavalry Corps, and I believe he was primarily responsible for it. Certainly it was a very sound organisation and, I think, was the best we ever had. The Cavalry Corps formed one dismounted division, commanded in turn by the three cavalry divisional commanders. This division consisted of three dismounted brigades, each found by one of the three cavalry divisions and commanded in turn by each of the three Brigadiers. Each dismounted brigade consisted of three dismounted battalions, one from each cavalry brigade, and commanded in turn by the three C.O.'s of regiments. A battalion comprised three companies, each found by a cavalry regiment and commanded by a Major or Captain. Each company consisted of six platoons (two from each squadron).

On the 3rd of January the 5th dismounted battalion, under, I think, Lieut.-Colonel Collins of the Greys, moved by train to Vermelles. The 20th Hussars Company was commanded by Captain Micholls, with Captain Beech second in command. " A " Squadron Platoons, Lieut. Read, Lieut. Balfour; " B " Squadron Platoons, Lieut. Goodhart, Lieut. F. Mann; " C " Squadron Platoons, Lieut. Thompson, Lieut. Sturt.

At Vermelles the battalion occupied huts, being in reserve. On the 7th January, Captain Micholls went to the infantry and Captain Darling took over the company. The other officers were also relieved from time to time from the regiment, and in his turn Colonel Cook and our R.H.Q. took command of the battalion. Our time was divided between reserve huts west of Vermelles, support trenches and dug-outs east of Vermelles, and front line trenches towards Hulloch.

This was all on ground that had been taken from the Germans during the Battle of Loos. Vermelles itself had been the scene of desperate fighting between the French and Germans for the possession of the " Château " of Vermelles. This so-called " château " was in reality a red brick villa. Hulloch was behind the German lines, and the front line trenches were about 100 yards apart. Our front line had been a German reserve line before the Battle of Loos. A feature of the sector was " The Hairpin," which consisted of two parallel saps that ran out towards the German lines. In reality, they were old German communication trenches. They were now blocked with sandbags, and we had bombing posts about twenty yards along them. A bit further on were the German bombing posts. Bombing had now become a great art, and the bombing officer and his merry men, who were all picked for their fighting qualities and their throwing, took a leading part in the scheme of defence. We were armed with the " Mills Bomb "; the Germans had got stick grenades. The soil was chalk, and once trenches were dug they needed very little revetting.

Our battalion headquarters enjoyed a very deep dug-out that had been bequeathed to us by the Boche. It was known that the Germans were doing a good bit of mining; in fact, they had already sprung some mines in this neighbourhood. We were just beginning to counter-mine, and had got some expert miners at work. While the company was in reserve, it sent up large working parties each night. These were employed chiefly in improving the second line trenches, doing carrying work for the miners, and trying to get some wire entanglements up, as none existed when we took over. Life in these trenches was fairly quiet but busy, as there always seemed to be lots of work to do in improving the trenches. We did what we could to annoy the Huns by sniping and bombing. There was also considerable artillery and trench mortar activity on both sides. In the latter department, the Boche were at this time a good bit ahead of us, and used to do a lot of damage to our trenches. They, however, inflicted very few casualties. Lieut. Jeffrey, " B " Squadron, who had recently joined from England, and was known as the " Iron Man," was of an inventive turn of mind, and had constructed some bomb slingers which were adopted. He was continually working at improving these weapons. Mention must also be made of the machine guns, which were now carefully organised in each sector and formed a great feature in the scheme of defence, by bringing cross fire to bear on threatened points. Some very good work was done by small patrols who went out at night and discovered what the Huns were up to.

There was no attack of any sort until the 13th of February. Major Little was then in command of the company. During the night of 13th-14th, we exploded a mine in front of the Hairpin. I think this was done chiefly to upset some of the German mining arrangements. Anyway, at about 9.30 p.m. on the 14th, the enemy exploded three mines in the same neighbourhood, making a line of craters across our front. They immediately made a bombing attack on the craters. Lieut. Hatton, who was our bombing officer, attacked simultaneously and drove the enemy back to the far lip of the crater. Lieut. Jeffrey also led a bombing attack up one leg of the Hairpin, and was killed there. Trench mortars were used to give covering fire, but were hopelessly short, and were requested to cease fire.

The machine guns did very good work by bringing flanking fire to bear along the edges of the crater. Our casualties, in addition to Lieut. Jeffrey, were seven men killed and two wounded. The regiment used 6,000 bombs during the night.

As the fighting died down, work was begun on the saps as these had been badly damaged. By the morning they were completely repaired. On the 15th we were relieved by some of the Essex Regiment, and all the cavalry were withdrawn from the trenches, the regiment going back to Fauquembergues.

It was about this time that Major Hurndall joined and took over " A " Squadron. He had gone to the Dardanelles with the Berkshire Yeomanry, and had then held a staff job.

During March, " Cavalry Corps " was done away with, each Cavalry Division being posted to an Army. The 2nd Cavalry Division went to the 2nd Army. Accordingly, early in April, we moved north from Fauquembergues to Licques, which was in the 2nd Army area, about fifteen miles east of Boulogne.

In March, Sergeant Beavon got a commission in the infantry and Mr. Austin in the regiment. Second Lieut. Austin was posted to " A " Squadron, S.S.M. Rabjohn

Chapter V.

became R.S.M. It was about this time that Major Sidney, Northumberland Yeomanry, joined us. He was attached to regimental headquarters. The summer of 1916 was spent by the cavalry in practising intensive " gap tactics." This was done in our case in a wide area of country that had been hired near St. Omer as training ground. On the 7th of June, the 5th Dismounted Battalion—in fact, I think the whole of the 2nd Dismounted Brigade—was hastily moved up by motor 'bus from Licques to Reninghelst. (Map 2.)

We went there in support of the Canadians, who had lost some trenches near Zillebeke, and had suffered heavy casualties. Lieut.-Colonel Cook and our R.H.Q. went up in charge of the 5th Battalion. We lived in tents at Reninghelst. The Canadian losses were made good with reinforcements, and on about the 18th June the Canadian Corps delivered a counter-attack during the night to get back the lost ground. We were to be used to consolidate or support the attack in the event of the Canadians being unable to complete the job alone. As a matter of fact, we were never even turned out of bed, for which we were very thankful, as it was a pouring wet night. The attack was a complete success, and all the lost ground was retaken. On the 20th June we returned to Licques by 'bus. All this time preparations had been going forward for the great offensive that was to be made on the Somme. The 2nd Army was denuded of troops to a great extent, and at the end of June our division marched to Vieux Berquin in the Hazebrouck area, where it was destined to remain as a mobile reserve to the 2nd Army.

We went to our old quarters at Vieux Berquin and Verte Rue. From here we sent parties to work in the mining operations that were going on near Kemmel. These had as their object the blowing up of the Messines Ridge. This was duly done a year later.

Each cavalry regiment now had more than its normal complement of men. Those over establishment could thus be spared for working parties of different sorts without interfering with the regiment as a mounted unit. On the 6th September, we left the 2nd Army for the Somme, where we were to join in a fresh offensive. (See Map 1.)

The dismounted party under Major Sidney went by train

to Carnoy (south-east of Albert), where they worked on the cavalry track by which we were to cross the trench system in our advance. On our way to the Somme we stopped on the 7th at Bermicourt, the 8th and 9th at Willencourt, the 10th at Occoches, doing a brigade scheme on the line of march. On the 11th we got to Naours, and on the 12th and 13th bivouacked near Bonnay. On the latter day, Commanding Officers and Squadron Leaders made a trip to the Somme battlefield, where the August offensive had already taken place. The historic Delville Wood and High Wood were visited. Thence a good view could be obtained of all the ground over which the cavalry were to advance if the next push was a success. On the 14th we arrived at our final camp about one mile north of Bray. On the 15th, 16th and 17th we stood to, ready to move, but nothing happened. Heavy rain set in and the camp became very wet and unpleasant. Between the 19th and 23rd, patrols were sent out under Lieuts. Bland, C. N. S. Woolf and P. S. Woolf, to get in touch with the infantry and find out the situation. One day, "B" Squadron went as far as Carnoy in case they should be wanted, but nothing occurred, and they came back again. (See Map 3.)

On the 2nd October, we moved a few miles west to a camp near Morlancourt. The weather seemed now to have definitely broken, and the camp soon got very wet. The "Cavalry Track" was almost impassable. The infantry and artillery found great difficulty in getting up ammunition, and we sent a number of pack horses to them to help in this connection. In addition, we had a working party away all the time. Both officers and men were continually relieved from the regiment.

We continued to practise "gap tactics," but it became increasingly obvious that cavalry would not be used before winter set in. At last the cavalry scheme was abandoned for the year, and on the 8th November we left "Mount Misery," as it had become known, for winter quarters. We spent successive nights in bivouac near Querrieu and Drucat, and finally reached our billets south of Hesdin. Regimental headquarters were at Wail, "B" Squadron at Wail and Galametz, "A" at Vieil Hesdin, and "C" at St. Georges.

Here we proceeded to make ourselves comfortable.

Chapter V.

General Chetwode had left the division and gone to Palestine, General Greenly taking his place. During the summer, Sergt. Gray had got a commission in the infantry, and had greatly distinguished himself at the Battle of the Somme, particularly at the taking of Le Sars.

In December, Lance-Sergt. Aston, Lance-Sergt. Bliss, Sergt. Clifford, Sergt. Cook and Lance-Sergt. Partridge all got commissions in the infantry.

Lieut.-Colonel G. T. R. Cook, D.S.O.

CHAPTER VI—1917, Arras and Lempire.

(See Maps I & III)

NEW Year's Day, 1917, found us still comfortably settled in the Wail-Vieil Hesdin area. Early in the New Year a hard frost set in which lasted for two months. As far as we were concerned, we thought it a good thing to get a long frost over during the war. Everyone hoped that one day victory, followed by peace, would bring with it a return to fox-hunting. We would rather, therefore, keep open winters for that blessed era, whenever it should come. On the 10th of January, the brigade, less 12th Lancers, moved nearer to the sea, partly so as to make use of the sands for mounted training. The 20th went to Nempont. Here billets were good, and, thanks to the hard weather, duck shooting was above the average. We were very comfortable, and were able to reach the sands for training. It was known that a great allied offensive was to take place in the spring, so we had once more to prepare to go through the " gap." Officially, the expression " gap " had long since been dropped, as it had become almost a term of derision. We had been told to speak of " operations beyond the trench system," or some such phrase. However, " gap " was shorter, and the term continued to be used to describe the cavalry's share in the offensive. A Divisional School was formed at Douriez, where officers and N.C.O.'s were taught the theory of this and other forms of open warfare. On the sands we tried to put this theory into practice. The scheme was briefly this :—The infantry were to break through the enemy's line. The cavalry were then to pass through them and advance as far as a definite objective that would be given them beforehand. German strong points were to be " masked," and passed by. Stragglers and those offering feeble resistance were to be mopped up. Once the

Chapter VI.

objective was reached, it was to be consolidated and held until the infantry came up. Patrols and covering parties only were to be pushed on further. We were not to pursue blindly whooping and yelling through the night, as the Prussian cavalry are said to have done after Waterloo. Nor were we to make raids on distant aerodromes, railway junctions and headquarters, as we were to have done on the Somme in 1916. Every detail was cut and dried, but I do not remember that anyone was told off to bring back the Kaiser's head on a charger. On the whole, it was a modest programme compared to former ones.

During the winter, a Divisional Football Cup, presented by General Greenly, was competed for. The regiment had a pretty hot team, captained by Corpl. Skeldon, "C" Squadron. We got into the final, where we met the 12th Lancers. We expected to win, as we had beaten the 12th most decisively early in the season. Since then we knew that they had re-organised and strengthened their team. If I remember right, our team lined up as follows :—*Goal*, Corpl. Moss; *backs*, Lance-Corpl. Skeldon, Pte. Grant; *half-backs*, Pte. Razzle, Corpl. Mountford, Pte. Davies; *forwards*, Pte. Boon, Corpl. Tuff, Pte. Yates, Pte. Blakeman, Saddler Corpl. Holden. The unexpected often happens in football, as in war, and the 12th gained a well-earned victory by three goals to two. General Kavanagh, commanding the Cavalry Corps, gave away the Cup and, in a short speech, suggested that we should soon be kicking something better than a football, or words to that effect. Anyway, everyone was optimistic about this coming offensive. One factor, however, caused us grave misgivings. There had been a great shortage of oats all through the winter. The daily ration had been reduced to six pounds per horse per day. Whether this was due to a real scarcity caused by the action of German submarines, or whether it was due to a groundless scare that there might be a scarcity, I do not know. I do know that the horses were not in the best condition for taking on heavy work. Those officers who had given their horses plenty of work so as to bring them "under the starter's orders" as it were, fit, had got them decidedly on the light side. These came in for unfavourable comments at horse inspections. Others had given their horses as little work as possible, and had shut them up in stuffy stables. These had the satisfaction of producing them sleek and comparatively fat at inspections. In the trial that was to come, it is my opinion that the hard thin horses triumphed over the soft, sleek ones. A story is told of Lieut. "Romulus" Woolf that at a horse inspection during the winter, the inspecting officer pointed to a horse in his troop and asked why it was thin. Romulus' answer was to ask another question: "Well, sir," he said, "if it comes to that, can you tell me why I am thin?" All who knew Romulus will realise that this question was unanswerable. In addition to short forage, the horses suffered at Nempont from a local form of low fever that pulled them down tremendously. I can only repeat that when we finally left for the battle, we were far from satisfied with the condition of the horses. That they came through as well as they did was only due to the untiring efforts of troop leaders, troop sergeants, and of the men themselves. It must be remembered that the weight of accoutrements had been greatly increased, and a Hussar in "marching order" weighed between eighteen and twenty stone.

Before getting on to the spring offensive, I must record some changes that took place in the regiment during the winter. Major Little went home for two months' duty with the 13th Reserve Regiment to supervise the training of young officers. Meanwhile, Major Sidney commanded " B " Squadron. On his return, Major Little went to regimental headquarters as second in command. Major Sidney was suddenly sent off to command a yeomanry regiment, who were taking part in following up the Germans in their withdrawal from the salient created by the Battle of the Somme. It will be remembered that they effected this withdrawal about February or March, 1917. They were followed up by the two Indian Cavalry Divisions and the Yeomanry Regiments who were doing Corps Cavalry in that area. Lieut. Hall relinquished the Adjutancy to take over " B " Squadron, vice Major Sidney, and became Temporary Captain. Lieut. Goodhart (second in command of " B ") became Adjutant, Lieut. Ogilvy from " C " going to " B " as second in command. Lieut. Peploe rejoined about this time from the 9th Signal Troop, and went to " A " Squadron as second in command. Lieut. MacIntyre had meanwhile gone to the 2nd Signal Squadron and Lieut. Wood-

Chapter VI.

man ("B" Squadron) had become signalling officer. Captain Barne, who had left us in 1915 to become Staff Captain, 4th Cavalry Brigade, had subsequently been appointed G.S.O. 2 2nd Cavalry Division. During the winter 1916-17, a Flying Corps Squadron had been formed, whose duty it would be to keep touch, during an advance, with the advanced troops of the cavalry. This squadron was directly under the G.O.C. Cavalry Corps. It was considered essential to have cavalry officers as observers, and even to have fairly senior officers. Volunteers were called for, and Seymour Barne, among others, answered the call, thus leaving a comfortable staff job.

We left Nempont for the battle on 5th April, and billeted that night at Fond de Val. The following officers started with the regiment :—

Lieut.-Col G. T. R. Cook, D.S.O., in Command.
Major A. C. Little, D.S.O., Second in Command.
Lieut. J. H. Goodhart, Adjutant.
Lieut. E. W. Brook, Signalling Officer.
Lieut. and Quartermaster W. Adams.
Lieut. R. J. Read, Intelligence Officer.

"A" Squadron.	"B" Squadron.	"C" Squadron.
Major F. B. Hurndall, M.C.	Capt. W. D. A. Hall, M.C.	Capt. J. C. Darling D.S.O.
Lieut. D. S. Peploe.	Lieut. W. W. Ogilvy.	Lieut. R. M. Thompson.
Lieut. P. S. Woolf (Remus).	Lieut. C. N. S. Woolf (Romulus).	Lieut. J. C. Bland.
Lieut. F. Wyborn.	Lieut. G. Glover.	Lieut. L. Groves.
Lieut. D. Jackson.	Lieut. L. Jones.	Lieut. C. K. Davy.
Lieut. Austin.	Lieut. Fairbrother.	Lieut. G. Cook.

The machine guns had, of course, long before this been formed into Machine Gun Squadrons. The 5th M.G. Squadron, under Major Martin, formed a unit in our brigade, Lieuts. F. Stout and Askin commanding the 20th Hussars sections. Before we actually went into action, Major Little was taken away and placed in the Cavalry Corps "pool" or "cage" of senior officers who were collected to be ready to replace casualties that might occur among commanding officers. We remained at Fond de Val all the 6th of April, and on the 7th marched to Outrebois. On the 8th we got to Grincourt-lez-Pas, fourteen miles south-west of Arras. This was to be more or less our jumping-off place for the offensive. We were housed in huts. Some of the horses were under open sheds, others were in the open. On the 9th we paraded in pouring rain. This sort of weather had come to be regarded as part and parcel of every big offensive by the Allies. In fact, it was by his conduct at this 1917 offensive that the clerk of the weather showed the world that he had definitely thrown in his lot with the Central Powers. We marched viâ Berles-au-Bois to Wailly. This was a deserted and much battered village that had been pretty close behind the line before the German withdrawal. We halted here for an hour, and gave the horses a feed; we were unable to water them. The more sagacious of them may, however, have scented from afar a battle and consequent water famine, and have lifted their heads and opened their mouths to receive a free drink from Jupiter Pluvius.

The march was continued viâ Ronville, which is just outside Arras, to "Telegraph Hill." I think we got on to the "Cavalry Track" practically from the moment we left Ronville. Telegraph Hill was a hill just west of Tilloy-les-Moufflains. I think I am right in saying that our infantry had taken it from the Germans that morning. Our attack had been a great success, but not apparently quite sufficiently so for the cavalry to be launched that night. There was very little shelling, but one shell fell in the rear troop (Lieut. Glover's) of "B" Squadron." Four men were wounded, and about six horses killed. Lieut. Glover himself was so shaken that he had to go sick a day or two later. The whole 2nd Cavalry Division was concentrated on Telegraph Hill by 4.15 p.m. The 3rd Cavalry Division were away to our left. Lieut. Wyborn went out with a patrol to get in touch with the infantry. At 8.30 p.m. we were ordered back to Wailly. It was, of course, dark by now. The clerk of the weather was doing his best for his allies by producing cold rain, sleet and snow. The cavalry track had been good as we advanced, but had already got very bad. In the dark it was impossible to avoid filled-in shell holes; these had become regular bog holes. A good many horses that got into them never got out again, but died there of cold and exhaustion. I have already referred to the condition of the horses. Any horse that recently had had fever and was not quite fit, or had not got his heart quite in the right place, once he got into a shell hole, just died there. It was particularly the common, under-bred horses that did this. We

Chapter VI.

spent a thoroughly wretched night, trekking along in the snow, numbed with cold, and suffering continual checks and jolts owing to congestion on the road. Wailly was reached at 3.30 a.m. on the 10th, and horses were pegged down in the snow. The men also were in the open.

About noon on the 10th we saddled up and moved off once more to Telegraph Hill, as it was hoped to push us through the gap that evening. At 5 p.m. the 3rd and 5th Cavalry Brigades were moved forward; I fancy on receipt of a report that Monchy had been taken. This was a commanding position on our left front. It was actually in the 3rd Cavalry Division sector, but it was realised that its capture was essential before the cavalry could be used. We trotted through Tilloy les Moufflains in column of route. We then formed " line of troop columns," and broke into a gallop. The Greys were on the right, 20th on the left, with the 12th following in support. The 3rd Cavalry Brigade was on our right. The regiment moved with " B " and " C " Squadrons in front and " A " in support. It was a fine sight, these large bodies of cavalry moving forward at a gallop over the open country, the columns closing in to pass through a defile where a gap in the wire had to be negotiated, and immediately deploying again when the obstacle was passed. Squadrons took the trenches in their stride. This time we really felt we were off, and expected shortly to be passing through the infantry, crossing the stream below Wancourt and occupying the ridge beyond. Patrols and advanced guards were all told off, and one word would be sufficient to despatch them on their missions. The spectacle of our advance was not lost to the Boche. He started shelling, and it quite looked as though we might be in for a warm reception. Then suddenly a snowstorm came on, blotting out everything. It had one good result—the shelling stopped. How the Brigadiers and C.O.'s kept their direction, I cannot say. Suffice it that they did. For our part, we merely followed the Colonel. Our immediate objective was a fold in the ground just behind the infantry front line. This fold was sufficient to hide us from view. It was to be used as a jumping-off place from which to go through the infantry. Suddenly, through the snow, a line of wire seemed to spring up in front of us—we came on it so unexpectedly, in fact, that some horses got their legs in it and the wire cutters had to be brought into play to get them out. We had reached our objective. About the same time the snowstorm stopped, but not before the ground had become well covered. We immediately got in touch with the infantry, and very soon found that the situation was not ripe for the cavalry. Our advance had so alarmed the Huns that their advanced patrols had been seen scurrying back to the main position. Here, however, they had got a strong line established. Our infantry were tired and cold, and were in no condition to press home a further attack. It was also discovered by a patrol, I think under Lieut. Wyborn, that Monchy had not been taken after all. The situation was reported to headquarters, and it was decided that we must spend the night where we were, in the hope of being able to advance the next morning. I think it is the opinion of most of us that this was the most uncomfortable night of the whole war. We were standing in several inches of mud with a covering of snow, a bitterly cold wind was blowing, and we were shelled intermittently all night. There could be no question of pegging down horses, so they were held, one man to two horses, while the other men got what rest and cover they could in shell holes. For the poor horses it was worse even than for the men. They had had no water for hours, they could not be off-saddled, and they were already very weak from exposure and short forage. No rations or forage came up to us, except a little that was fetched by a party with pack horses who went back under Lieut. Davy to a Divisional Dump. The wretched pack horses had an awful journey in the dark through the heavy going, and some were too exhausted to get back to us at all.

During the night a German counter-attack was expected. Some machine guns and Hotchkiss rifles were sent up from the brigade to strengthen the line. Lieut. "Remus" Woolf and a dismounted patrol also spent the night in a shell hole in front of the infantry, so as to keep the Brigadier quite " au_fait " with the situation. During the night the Boche regained some ground on a hill away to our right front. When dawn broke, the leading regiments of the brigade were more or less under cover in our friendly fold in the ground, but the 12th and " E " Battery R.H.A., who were in rear, were in view of the Huns, and soon came under machine gun fire. The shelling was also increasing. So there the brigade stood in the open, as it had done all night—hungry, tired, frozen to the marrow, and under fire from an enemy to whom we were unable to reply, for he was safely underground and not a man was showing. The steadiness of the troops was admirable. At last it was realised that there was no immediate prospect of an advance, and that we were suffering casualties to no useful purpose. At 8 a.m., the order came to retire towards Tilloy. In so doing we had to cross very open ground, and were shelled to a certain extent. The discipline of the men remained magnificent. Lieuts. Wyborn and Woolf stayed out with patrols, the former mounted on the left flank and the latter dismounted where he had been during the night. All day they both continued to send in valuable information. About 1 p.m. the 5th Brigade was relieved by the 4th Brigade, and moved back into Divisional Reserve on Telegraph Hill. At 5 p.m. the whole division was withdrawn. We reached Wailly at 6.15 p.m. The horses were picketted in the same muddy field as before, but this time cover was found for the men among the ruined houses. Our casualties amounted to Lieuts. Ogilvy and Glover and five men wounded. One man died, 37 horses were killed or died of exhaustion. The whole brigade lost 477 horses, so we really got off very lightly. On the 12th we moved back to Grincourt, where we at once began to refit, and to cast horses that would not be fit for work for some time. Some remounts joined. The following letter was received by the Brigadier from the Divisional Commander (General Greenly), dated 10th April :—" I wish to express to you and all ranks of your command my admiration of the behaviour of the 5th Cavalry Brigade yesterday and to-day under most trying conditions. Your support to the infantry was of great value to the general situation at a time which without you might at any moment have become critical in the event of a counterattack." The Brigadier added to these remarks : "The Brigadier, while deeply regretting the losses sustained by the brigade, wishes to place on record his keen appreciation of the fine soldierly conduct and high standard of discipline displayed by all officers, N.C.O.'s and men."

It soon became apparent that there would be no opportunity for the employment of cavalry in the Arras battle. The

Cavalry Corps was accordingly withdrawn to comfortable billets. On the 20th April, the regiment moved to the area Outrebois, Mezerolles, Barly. Here we devoted ourselves to getting the horses back into condition. Forage, which had been so scarce all the winter, suddenly became plentiful. The young grass was also growing, and troop and squadron leaders scoured the countryside to find the best grazing they could, much as Ahab, king of Israel, is said once to have done. Troops then went to exercise independently, and horses got the benefit of the patches of grass that had been discovered along the lanes, the edges of woods, or dry water courses. On 23rd April, Captain Barne, M.C., was shot down and killed while serving with the Flying Corps. By his death the regiment, and indeed the Army, lost one who was indeed an ideal cavalry officer. Seymour Barne might well have been taken as an example of what a cavalry officer should be. He was a consummate horseman, and under all circumstances, in peace and in war, was absolutely fearless. Yet there was none of the traditional " beau sabreur " about him. He was one of the most unassuming and modest of men. In action he was cool and collected to a degree, and was possessed of excellent judgment. He was a sportsman to the backbone, he loved the regiment, and was himself beloved alike by officers and men. On the 6th May Captain Silvertop rejoined and went to " C " Squadron as second in command, Lieut. Thompson going from " C " to " B." By the end of April the horses were rapidly recovering from the effects of what they had been through, and early in May the Cavalry Corps took over a portion of the front line east of Peronne. We left the Outrebois area on the 12th of May, and on the 15th we arrived at Tincourt. (See Map 3.) This was a village most of which had been destroyed by the Huns during their retirement early in the year. We had a very comfortable camp just outside a wood about a mile from the village. The weather was on the whole very good, and this was in many ways much more comfortable than the usual billets with their perpetual " reclamations " and other worries. The horses prospered and enjoyed almost unlimited grazing. On the 17th May a trench party, consisting of fourteen officers and 324 other ranks, under Major Little, went up to Lempire, a few miles away, where they went into reserve billets. These

Chapter VI.

consisted of cellars among the ruins of the village. While the Cavalry Corps held this line, they did so by means of a number of detached posts, not a continuous trench line. Each post was held by about a squadron. While the regiment was in reserve, the usual working parties were supplied nightly for work in the front line. On 24th May, squadrons went into the front line, regimental headquarters remaining at Lempire. The sector was a quiet one, but on the 26th Lempire was heavily shelled and " A " Squadron also had some casualties. The German line was actually a sort of outpost line in front of the much talked about Hindenburg Line. The wire of that famous line could be seen from our posts. Patrols went out into No Man's Land most nights to see what the Boche was up to. On the 29th a patrol, under Lieut. Davy, brought in some useful information as to the enemy's activities. On the 31st, the 20th were relieved by the 16th Lancers, and went back into reserve at Lempire. On the 3rd of June Captain Smith, R.A.M.C., the regimental M.O., and a very popular one, was wounded. On the 7th of June we relieved the 16th once more. During the night of the 9th-10th the Greys, who were on our left, made a very successful raid on Gillemont Farm, which was a ruin held by the Germans. On the 10th there was considerable shelling by the enemy in retaliation, and the regiment suffered a few casualties. On the 14th we were relieved by the 16th Lancers, and went into support. On the 15th, the 20th were withdrawn altogether, their place in support being taken by the 3rd Hussars.

The regiment went back to the horses near Tincourt for ten days' mounted training. The following day Major Hurndall went off on a staff job, and Lieut. Peploe took over " A " Squadron. Lieut. Woodman became 2nd in command of "A" Squadron. On the 27th a party from the regiment went up to Lempire again. It consisted of fourteen officers and 338 other ranks, under Colonel Cook. The Colonel took command of the sector, which was occupied by three squadrons of the 20th and two squadrons of the Oxford Yeomanry. On the 28th we took over the front line from the 3rd Hussars. The trenches were very wet as the result of violent thunder storms, and there was plenty of work to be done baling and pumping them dry. A continuous line of wire had now been constructed in front of the posts, but these had not been connected up by trenches. Our patrols were more active than the enemy's, and during their nightly wanderings in No Man's Land they had the place to themselves. On the 4th of July, the 20th were relieved by the 3rd Hussars and went into support, on the 5th Major Sidney took over from Colonel Cook, and the following day the cavalry were relieved by infantry. On the 12th we left Tincourt and returned to the Outrebois-Barly area, stopping on the way at Suzanne, Morlancourt, Thievres, Estrée Wamin. On the 27th and 28th there was a Divisional Horse Show at Frévent. The horses had profited very much from their time in the Tincourt area, and I think this show demonstrated that the division was now once more fit for any task they might be called upon to perform. On the 1st of August there was a re-organisation of signallers. These were taken from squadrons and collected at regimental headquarters as a "Signal Troop." On the 21st Lieut. Sturt left us, going to the Cadet School at Netheravon as an instructor. Intensive training was now carried out, as the corn had been cut and mounted troops could get about on the stubble fields. Anti-gas measures became a great feature. In order to get all ranks quite familiar with their box respirators, these instruments of torture had to be worn by everyone for half an hour daily, whatever they were doing. Thus it might well happen that at Squadron Orderly Room a prisoner (I beg his pardon, "an accused") might quake in his boots and box respirator in front of a Squadron Leader who was endeavouring to "tell him off," without dimming his eye-pieces or shifting his nose-clip. Witnesses would also be in a similar state while telling "the truth, the whole truth, and nothing but the truth." If the "Sanitary Man" made as an excuse, for letting the incinerator out, the statement that he could not see out of his respirator, this was merely taken to indicate that he required more practice. He should, if justice were done, accordingly be made to incinerate in his respirator for an hour daily instead of half an hour. Towards the end of September a working party, comprising Captain Silvertop, Lieut. Leslie Jones, Lieut. Lethbridge and 108 other ranks, went to Les Brebis; Major Sidney commanded the party (styled a battalion) found by the whole brigade. Early in October, a big offensive was launched

Chapter VI.

by our 2nd and 5th Armies in the area east of Ypres. There were some hopes of employing the cavalry, and we accordingly moved towards the battle. This time we were, I fancy, the rear brigade of the Cavalry Corps in the order of battle. Consequently, we never got further than Siracourt, near St. Pol. On the 8th October Lieut. Galbraith, who was now on the staff, went to Egypt, and on the 18th Captain Peploe was struck off, sick. Captain Sanford, who had been wounded while serving with the infantry, rejoined us about this time and took over " B " Squadron vice Captain Hall, who took over " A." We now moved south into winter quarters, stopping on the 18th at Grand Bouret and Petit Bouret, on the 19th at Montrelet, Fieffres and Bonneville. On the 20th October we reached our allotted area at Wailly, Loeuilly and Tilloy (south of Amiens). Here we made ourselves very comfortable. About this time merit was recognised, and Lieut. and Quartermaster Bill Adams was promoted Captain. On the 4th November, the O.C. "C" Squadron went home for the winter to help train officers with the 5th Reserve Cavalry Regiment. Captain Silvertop took over " C " Squadron, Lieut. Bland becoming second in command.

CHAPTER VII—Battle of Cambrai, (November 1917).

THE regiment was not destined to remain quietly in winter quarters for long. The Cavalry Corps was to take part in General Byng's famous attack in the direction of Cambrai. The 5th Cavalry Brigade moved on 15th November, the regiment marching viâ Rumigny, Boves and Aubigny to Le Hamel (Map 3), where they arrived shortly before 8 p.m. On the 16th the march was continued at 3 p.m. It was a very slow and tiring march, and it was 2 a.m. on the 17th before the destination was reached, some huts on the old Somme battlefield. At this time there were on the strength of the regiment a large number of "dismounted" officers and men. These enabled the regiment to find a working party and still to be at full strength as a mounted unit. I referred to this arrangement on the Somme in 1916. All surplus officers and men left the mounted unit on the 19th November, when a further advance was to be made. "B" Echelon was also left behind. The following is a list as far as I can get it of the officers who accompanied the regiment to the battle :—

    Lieut.-Colonel G. T. R. Cook, D.S.O., in Command.
    Major A. C. Little, D.S.O., Second in Command.
    Capt. J. H. Goodhart, M.C., Adjutant.
    Lieut. C. Woodman, Signalling Officer.
    Lieut. E. W. Brook, Intelligence Officer.
    Capt. W. Adams, Quartermaster.

"A" Squadron.	"B" Squadron.	"C" Squadron.
Capt. Hall, M.C.	Capt. Sanford.	Capt. Silvertop, M.C.
Lieut. Thompson.	Lieut. C. N. S. Woolf.	Lieut. Cooper Bland.
Lieut. P. S. Woolf.	Lieut. Clinton, M.C.	Lieut. Taylor.
Lieut. Wyborn, M.C.	Lieut. L. Jones.	Lieut. Groves.
Lieut. Austin.	Lieut. Ralli.	Lieut. Davy.
Lieut. Jackson.		Lieut. Cook.

The brigade marched at 1 a.m. on the 20th, and reached its position of assembly north of Saulcourt at 6.20 a.m. This

Chapter VII.

was "zero hour" for the attack.

It will be remembered that this attack was carried out very largely by the use of tanks on a big scale. There was no preliminary bombardment; the tanks had been assembled behind the line without the Boche finding it out, and at zero hour they just walked over the top. This took the unsuspecting Huns completely by surprise, and at first the attack was a great success. A few days before there had been a secret demonstration of the effect of tanks on wire entanglements. They drove great holes through the wire, and the infantry were enabled to advance with comparative ease. It was then hoped to pour the cavalry through the gap, and complete the defeat of the bewildered enemy. If the cavalry reached their final objectives they would be established on both sides of Cambrai, which place would then fall into our hands. At noon the situation warranted a further advance, and the regiment moved to just south of Gouzeaucourt. They then marched west of that village by the cavalry track to a position one and a half miles south of Masnieres. It was a very wet evening, and the brigade had to spend the night here in the mud and the rain. At midnight an order came to move back, but this was quickly cancelled and the rest of the night was spent in this very uncomfortable position. At dawn on the 21st, the regiment sent out two officers' patrols to discover the exact situation. These patrols reported that British troops were holding Masnieres, but that the enemy had still got Couvrecouer. At 2 p.m. the brigade advanced towards Masnieres, expecting to go through the infantry and seize the next objective. About this time, however, a heavy German counter-attack developed against the bridgehead held by our troops at Masnieres. This put all idea of mounted action out of the question for the moment. In the evening the brigade was ordered back to north of Saulcourt. It was a very unpleasant march in the dark. The cavalry track had got very bad from the heavy rain, and old telephone wires, etc., proved to be serious obstacles to mounted troops. Lieut. Davy's horse got a wire round its legs while the regiment was dismounted at a halt, and in his efforts to get free he kicked Lieut. Davy, breaking his arm. The horses were watered at Hendecourt, this being the first water they had had for 40 hours. The bivouac was reached at 10 p.m. On the

22nd, it seemed that the attack was held up, and that there would be no opportunity for the employment of cavalry. Orders were received for billeting parties to get ready. These orders were, however, shortly cancelled. The only cavalry who had been employed so far in the battle were some of the Canadian Cavalry Brigade. These had made a very gallant advance east of Masnieres, and had put some German guns out of action. I believe a tank, in trying to cross the canal, then broke the bridge behind them. Anyway, the Canadians suffered very heavy casualties indeed.

The regiment remained north of Saulcourt all the 22nd ready to support any threatened point in the line. I don't think there was much prospect on this day of cavalry being employed in any other way. On the 23rd, the brigade marched to a camp near Fins. They did not get there till long after dark; in fact, I think it was about 10 p.m. The 24th was a cold, wet, and thoroughly uncomfortable day. No move was made, the brigade being at one hour's notice.

On the 25th, the whole of the 2nd Cavalry Division marched to south-east of Ribecourt. Here orders were issued for the 4th Cavalry Brigade to make a dismounted attack northwards from Bourlon Village. The 3rd and 5th Cavalry Brigades were to be ready to exploit the success of this attack mounted. This certainly sounded a most optimistic programme —that a force of the same strength as a weak infantry battalion should be expected to achieve such a success that two whole cavalry brigades could hope to be employed in completing the victory. These orders were, however, cancelled during the day, and instead the division had to form three dismounted battalions, one from each brigade. The 5th Cavalry Brigade found a battalion consisting of twenty-two officers and 600 other ranks under the command of Lieut.-Col. Collins, Royal Scots Greys. The company formed from the regiment comprised five officers and 218 other ranks, under Captain Silvertop. The battalion remained for the moment near Ribecourt, under the orders of the 40th Division. The horses were taken back to camp at Fins. With their departure departed also all hope of the regiment's being employed mounted. The offensive had followed roughly on the lines of its predecessors. The attack had at first been a great success,

Chapter VII.

the cavalry had been moved up and had been within an ace of being employed on a large scale. Then had come heavy German counter-attacks. Our infantry had been pinned to their ground, and had been unable to advance further. In places they had even had to give up some of the positions that had been so hardly won. They were now fighting hard, but in what had become a defensive action. On this particular day, that greatest of all enemies of Allied offensives, the clerk of the weather, produced a bit of November at its worst—heavy snow fell during the afternoon to add to the discomfort already caused by wet and cold. These discomforts were, as usual, borne by all ranks in the most cheerful spirit. There was considerable shelling of the ground east of Ribecourt, and the Medical Officer (Captain Cleveland) and nine other ranks were wounded, this being our second M.O. to become a casualty within a few months. The company remained in the same position until the evening of the 26th, when they moved to reserve dug-outs just south of Flesquieres. During the night the 40th Division were relieved by the 62nd Division. The 5th Dismounted Battalion became attached to this latter division, and at 6 a.m. on the 27th were moved to reserve trenches on the east side of the Canal Du Nord west of Graincourt. During the day, the 4th Dismounted Battalion was attached to the 185th Infantry Brigade, the 3rd and 5th Dismounted Battalions to the 186th Infantry Brigade. Both these brigades were in the 62nd Division. In the evening all three battalions took over front-line trenches. The sector allotted to the 5th Battalion was at the head of a small re-entrant in the northern part of Bourlon Wood. This wood had at one time during the battle been entirely in our hands. Then there had been heavy fighting there during the German counter-attacks, and on the night in question we held most of it, but the Germans held the northern end. The regiment took over from some of the West Riding Regiment. There was considerable shelling during the relief, and Captain Silvertop, M.C., was killed. The two Lieuts. Woolf were both wounded, Lieut. C.N.S. Woolf dying in hospital soon afterwards.

The relief was completed about midnight, 27th-28th, the left being in touch with the 12th Lancer Company, the right with a battalion of Scots Guards. The trenches were shallow and were not continuous. However, by now the cavalryman had become pretty useful with his pick and shovel, and by the morning a good continuous line had been dug, and this in spite of continual annoyance from Boche machine guns.

Throughout the 28th the position was subjected to heavy shell fire from the Huns; this became intense from 3 p.m. to 7 p.m., and from 8 p.m. to midnight. No attack was, however, made. The casualties in the regiment during the 27th and 28th amounted, in addition to the three officers mentioned above, to five other ranks killed and twenty-four other ranks wounded. In Captain Silvertop and Lieut. C. N. S. Woolf we lost two very gallant officers. The former had been wounded in 1914, and had never properly recovered the use of one arm. He had, however, insisted on rejoining the regiment. Lieut. Woolf was one of the host of civilians who volunteered for service the moment war broke out, and who soon made himself a very efficient officer.

At 4 a.m. on the 29th the 5th dismounted Battalion was relieved by a battalion of the London Regiment, the 5th Machine Gun Squadron being left in the line. Lieut. Groves went to hospital suffering from gas. The horses had been sent up from Fins and met the trench party at Flesquieres. They then rode back to Fins. The following message was received from General Greenly, commanding the 2nd Cavalry Division :—

"General Sir Julian Byng, commanding 3rd Army, has just paid a personal visit to the division in order to express his warmest thanks to the troops and his appreciation of the valuable services they have rendered, especially in their defence of Bourlon Wood."

The morning of the 30th was devoted to baths, which had been arranged at Fins. Suddenly at 11 a.m. an urgent order was received to turn out at once, as it was reported that the enemy had broken through between Masnieres and Epehy, that is on the southern flank of the salient created by our advance, and that they had occupied Gouzeaucourt. The 5th Cavalry Brigade were ordered to seize and hold the high ground between Revelon Farm and a point south-west of Gouzeaucourt. Colonel Cook heard this order from an officer of the *Divisional Staff* who was on his way to Brigade Headquarters.

Chapter VII.

He accordingly gave the order to saddle up at once. In an incredibly short time the regiment was on parade. Without waiting for the rest of the brigade the Colonel moved off at once towards Gouzeaucourt, at the same time sending our four patrols to find out the exact situation. From their reports it was ascertained that on a ridge west (that is short of) the brigade's objective there was a line of trenches which was very thinly held by the 470th Company Royal Engineers. The Huns were 300 yards beyond. The C.O. at once re-inforced the R.E. with the whole regiment. The Brigadier then ordered an advance. The regiment made a dismounted advance of about 1,000 yards, killing the Germans encountered en route. Before long the 2nd Battalion Coldstream Guards, advancing from the direction of Metz-en-Couture, joined in on the left of the 20th. The objective, a ridge south of Gouzeaucourt, was reached, but a further advance was prevented by heavy enfilade fire from the north. The whole line was, however, established from the eastern exit of Gouzeaucourt to Revelon Farm. The 5th Cavalry Brigade was withdrawn in the evening, except the 20th, who remained in the front line all night, and for one Squadron of Greys, who stayed to support them. The right of the regiment was in touch with Hodson's Horse, belonging to one of the Indian Cavalry Divisions, but on our left there was a considerable gap on the right of the Coldstream Guards. Major Little collected the remnants of three Companies of Infantry who seemed to have lost all their officers, and with these he filled the gap. For his action throughout this day he was awarded a bar to his D.S.O. During the night the regiment consolidated the line of a sunken road and a continuous trench line was dug. At 5.30 a.m. on the 1st December Hodson's Horse and the 11th Battalion Middlesex Regiment between them took over the front held by the 20th, as well as the bit on the left up to the Coldstream Guards. By 7.15 a.m. the 20th were back in camp, very well satisfied with their share in the recapture of Gouzeaucourt. The Brigade stood to saddled up till 4 p.m. Then a working party was found to dig a support line south-west of Gouzeaucourt. The Regiment's contribution consisted of two officers and 100 other ranks. Throughout the 2nd and 3rd December the 5th Cavalry Brigade " stood to " at half an hour's notice ready to act either mounted in the event of a German attack from the direction of Epehy, or as a dismounted battalion to support the 1st Cavalry Division, who were now in the line south-east of Gouzeaucourt. A working party was found each night to dig trenches. On the 4th December a dismounted company was found by the regiment, Captain Sanford being in command. They were in support to some of the 1st Cavalry Division near Revelon Farm. This had now become a quiet spot, and on the 5th they were withdrawn, being back in camp by 10 p.m.

On the 6th the regiment marched south to Cartigny—here " B " Echelon rejoined. The men were accommodated in huts and tents, the horses in open stables. On the 7th the march was continued to Glisy, just east of Amiens. Here the regiment got back from the battle area to civilisation. The men were in houses and barns, the horses in the open. On the 8th the regiment got to Hornoy (H.Q., " A " and " B ") and Vraignes (" C ") (north-west of Amiens). The following message was received from the Divisional Commander :—
" I wish to congratulate all ranks of the Division upon the admirable way in which you met the many and varied demands made upon you during the recent operations. Fighting, work, continuous exposure and want of rest were all carried through with a courage and determination which no troops could surpass, and I wish once again to record my deepest admiration and appreciation of your conduct and services. I wish also to congratulate all concerned, but especially the Squadron and Troop Leaders, upon the present condition of the horses : the fact that they have maintained their efficiency as they have is not only the best proof of the good working condition in which you produced them, but also the best reward for the unremitting work and care previously devoted to them."

On the 18th December the Dismounted Company, under Capt. Sanford left the regiment once more to take its place in the trenches. They went by lorry to Saleux, a few miles south-west of Amiens, and by rail from there to Roisel, east of Peronne, marching to billets at Vendelles. They took over front line trenches from the 8th Battalion Royal West Kents on the 20th December. These trenches were in Cote Wood. They remained in the area, being alternately in the front line

Chapter VII.

and in support, until the 29th January, 1918, when they rejoined the regiment at Hornoy and Vraignes. Things had been very quiet on the part of the front held by the Brigade, and casualties had been very light. On 5th January Captain Sanford was promoted Major.

CHAPTER VIII—Spring and Summer 1918.

The German Offensive.

(See Map III).

EARLY in February the Cavalry Corps moved up into the forward area of the 5th Army, which was on the right of the British line. The regiment left Hornoy on 4th February and marched to the area Bovelles—Ferrieres—Guignemicourt. On the 5th they got to Harbonnieres, and on the 6th to Athies, south of Peronne. This was a ruined village where a few houses had been repaired. The men were in huts and the horses in open stables. Here the 20th remained until the 4th of March. All this time they were ready to turn out at short notice as the 2nd Cavalry Division were Mobile Reserve to the Cavalry Corps.

On the 5th March a dismounted company of 224 all ranks under Captain Hall went to Vermand, north-west of St. Quentin. They were employed in constructing trenches and wire entanglements. It was known by now that a heavy German attack might soon be expected on this part of the line, and these were efforts to put the " battle zone " in a proper state of defence. The dismounted company rejoined on the 11th March, and on the 13th the regiment marched via Ham to Quesnoy. They were accommodated in tents in the Bois D'Autecourt. The weather was glorious and everyone was very comfortable. On the 13th Captain Thompson went to England, sick, and Lieut. Woodman became 2nd in command of " A " Squadron. On the 14th the Brigade was organised as a " Dismounted Brigade Group " under Colonel Cook, for employment, in the event of a hostile attack, in accordance with the 3rd Corps Defence Scheme. It will be observed that the scheme seemed to be from the first to employ the cavalry

Chapter VIII.

as infantry. There seems to have been no idea of utilising the Cavalry Corps as a mounted unit. On the 18th March a working party of four officers and 150 other ranks went to Jussy. Major Little was in command of the Brigade party. It may be mentioned that General Campbell was in hospital in England and was known to be very ill indeed. Colonel Collins (Greys) was commanding the 5th Brigade.

On the 20th March the warning was received to " Prepare for attack." On the morning of the 21st, Jussy was heavily bombarded, and it was found necessary to move the troops clear of the village. Major Little's party was increased by the addition of men of other units who had become detached in the retirement that on this fateful day had taken place from the front line. During the day the remainder of the 5th Brigade Dismounted Party arrived under Colonel Cook, and the whole force was concentrated at Lizerolles. A line was taken up on the outskirts of Montescourt, facing east, with units of the 43rd Infantry Brigade on both flanks. The 54th Infantry Brigade also arrived from the south and dug in facing north. Orders were received in the evening that the whole of this part of the line was to start to retire at midnight 21st-22nd, and to cross the Crozat Canal, the retirement being covered by the 5th Dismounted Brigade. For some reason these brigades had now become known as " Dismounted Brigades," not " Dismounted Battalions," which was really all they were. I shall, however, stick to the term used in the War Diary and call them brigades.

On the 22nd the 3rd and 5th Dismounted Brigades were both under Brig.-General Bell Smythe (the G.O.C. 3rd Cavalry Brigade), and were at the disposal of the 14th Division. The whole force had retired behind the Canal by 4.15 a.m. on the 22nd without being molested. They then marched south-west to Faillouel, where they arrived about 6 a.m. At 1.45 p.m. the 5th Dismounted Brigade moved to a sandpit between Faillouel and Jussy, where they were in support to the 43rd Infantry Brigade, and were held in readiness to counter attack if the enemy should cross the canal. It was known that the bridges had not been thoroughly destroyed. During the evening the Germans got across at Mennessis and got into Jussy. No counter attack was ordered, but the Brigade remained in close support of the infantry, eight machine guns being posted to the south of Jussy. During the night parties were sent from the Brigade to re-inforce the infantry, and at 3 a.m. on the 23rd the situation was as follows :—The Germans were in Jussy. The 20th Hussars and half the Greys were on a railway embankment south of Jussy, under the orders of the O.C. 9th Scottish Rifles. The eight machine guns were still south of Jussy. One squadron of the 12th Lancers was still at the sandpit and one squadron were about to move to some high ground west of Faillouel as escort to some guns that were in position there. The remainder of the 12th, Greys, and 5th Machine Gun Squadron were echeloned back on the right flank and were east of the Faillouel—Jussy road. At 6 a.m. the infantry reported that they had made a local counter attack and had cleared Jussy of the enemy. It was a foggy morning and it was difficult to find out the exact situation. The Huns were, however, not far away and kept up a heavy bombardment with trench mortars throughout the night and early morning.

By 8 a.m. they had reached the line of the railway south of Jussy and were reported to have broken through further to the right near Mennessis. At 11.30 a.m. Major Little was sent to collect stragglers of various units along the Faillouel—Flavy Le Martel road and to take up a position there. One squadron of the Greys, one squadron of the 12th, and one regiment of the 4th Dismounted Brigade were ordered to join him there. Major Little soon had quite a nice little army collected and made up his mind to counter attack the line of the railway. Just as he was launching his attack the fog lifted and a continuous stream of Germans was seen to be pouring round the left flank, which was completely in the air. The counter attack was abandoned and the exposed left flank thrown back to meet this threat of envelopment. The line of the Faillouel—Flavy road was then held successfully for two hours. At the end of that time the Brigade was ordered to concentrate on Faillouel. Here touch was gained on the right with the 4th Dismounted Brigade. The left was still in the air. About 3 p.m. the enemy once more discovered this gap and started to pour infantry through it. A retirement was accordingly ordered to the edge of a large wood south-west of Faillouel. At 4 p.m. some French troops came up in support

Chapter VIII.

and finally the Brigade was withdrawn through them to the line Cugny—Ugny Le Cay, where some of our infantry had dug themselves in. The Brigade was then further withdrawn to La Neuville En Beine, where they went into billets for the night. On this day, 23rd March, an attempt was made to form some sort of a mounted force out of the Cavalry. From the men left with the horses of the 2nd Cavalry Division 100 per brigade were formed into a regiment under Captain Bonham, of the Greys. The remainder of the horses and transport of the 5th Cavalry Brigade moved to the Bois De Carlepont, near Pontoise, arriving there at 7.30 p.m.

On the 24th the led horses and transport moved south-west to a bivouac near Bailly. Horses were sent from the 5th Brigade to try and pick up the 5th Dismounted Brigade. The latter were meanwhile marching from La Neuville, where we had left them on the evening of the 23rd, north-west to Beaumont-en-Beine. Here both the 4th and 5th Dismounted Brigades remained in support of the 43rd Infantry Brigade, who were to be relieved at noon by French troops. It was again a foggy morning. The orders for the 4th and 5th Brigades were to cover the retirement of the 43rd Brigade and themselves to retire when this brigade had passed through them. This happened at 12.45 p.m., and at 1 p.m. the 4th and 5th Brigades began to retire. It was then found that the French, who were supposed to be relieving the British, were themselves retiring. There had evidently been some misunderstanding. The G.O.C. 43rd Infantry Brigade accordingly ordered the two dismounted brigades to occupy the high ground east of Beines. Here they joined some French troops and the position was held until 4 p.m., when orders were received to retire on Buchoire. At 6 p.m. an order was received from General Greenly, who had now taken over command of the 14th Division, to make a further retirement to Crisolles. The French had taken over this part of the line, and our troops in retiring passed through French guns in action. Our men had now done a lot of marching and a certain amount of fighting with but very little rest, and all were pretty tired. The march had, however, to be continued over the dry canal that ran between Noyon and Nesle to Beaurains. They arrived here at midnight and found their horses, which had been sent there for them.

During the night this force was organised into two regiments, the 4th Brigade finding one regiment under Captain Herman (Carabiniers) and the 5th Brigade another under Major Little. The whole was put under Colonel Cook and was to be known as "Cook's Detachment." One troop of the 5th Lancers was also included in the detachment. There were rather more horses than men. The spare horses were sent to Noyon. The detachment moved off at 6 a.m. on the 25th, and marched to Vauchelles. Here they got in touch with the 14th Division, who were at Beaurains and Sermaize, with a cavalry detachment under General Harman (G.O.C. 3rd Cavalry Division) that was at Lagny, and with some French troops who were holding Noyon and to the north of it. It was found that the French were holding Bussy, Crizolles, and Autrecourt strongly, the situation seemed well in hand, and in the opinion of the G.O.C. 3rd Corps Noyon was considered to be safe for the present.

At 2.10 p.m. orders were received for Cook's Detachment to join General Harman at Lagny. This was done at 5.30 p.m. The detachment was then organised as a dismounted company of 250 rifles, and moved off to take over posts in the front line east of Le Chapitre Wood. This wood is east of Campagne. Soon after starting, a request came from the French for immediate support near Cattigny. Accordingly all the cavalry under General Harman's orders rejoined their horses and moved mounted in that direction. It was dark by the time they arrived south-west of Cattigny. Here they took up a defensive position for the night. At 1 a.m. on the 26th they were ordered to move south-west to a bleak and bare bit of ground between Dives and Lassigny. At 9.30 a.m. Cook's Detachment re-crossed the Divette stream and, in conjunction with some French troops, held a semi-circular line from a wood north of Cuy, through a farm north of this wood, to the junction of Culagny and Scéancourt. The right was in touch with the 3rd Cavalry Division Detachment, who were at Cuy, and a few of the Northumberland Hussars were holding some high ground north-west of Lagny. At 10.45 a.m. the French withdrew from Lagny. The 20th and one squadron of the 16th Lancers then worked up the main street of the village dismounted and established themselves half-way along it. The

Chapter VIII.

Greys advanced on the left and linked up with the Northumberland Hussars, and the G.O.C. 10th French Division collected what troops he could at Plessis and Cacheleux and advanced to a wooded hill north-west of Lagny. A further advance was at first contemplated, but this was counter ordered. At 3 p.m. a large body of the enemy were observed to be assembling for an attack from the direction of the Bois Des Essarts. There were French troops intermingled with ours along most of the front held by the cavalry, and both sides were in Lagny. It was then discovered that the enemy had found a gap in our line somewhere on the wooded hills to the north and that he was pouring troops round our left flank. We had no reserves available either to counter attack or to fill the gap, and therefore there was nothing for it but to retire in order to avoid being cut off. A retirement was accordingly ordered to a position covering the crossings over the stream at Dives. This position was held until 5 p.m., when the enemy again succeeded in turning the left flank, and a further retirement became necessary, the detachment receiving orders to move to Thiescourt. The withdrawal was carried out under very heavy artillery fire, which was directed especially on the exits from Dives. The regiment suffered some casualties, and among them was Colonel Cook, who was killed. From Thiescourt the party marched to Elincourt, where they rejoined General Harman. On the 27th they received orders to return to the 2nd Cavalry Division. They marched south via Coudun to Venette, just west of Compiegne, where they arrived at 1.30 p.m., and found the rest of the 5th Cavalry Brigade. Units were immediately sorted out from the various detachments, the brigade going to near Canly for the night. The regiment went to Arsy.

I cannot leave this phase of the operations without referring to the great loss sustained by the regiment in the death of the Commanding Officer. Colonel Cook, D.S.O., during his command, had proved himself a good organiser and a good leader. In billets he was untiring in his efforts to bring to perfection every detail both in organisation and in training. In action he was a sound and fearless leader. I doubt whether sufficient credit has ever been paid to his quick appreciation and prompt action on the occasion of the counter attack at Gouzeaucourt, during the Battle of Cambrai. In his handling of

"Cook's Detachment" he displayed that tact and judgment which are so essential when an officer is commanding a mixed force composed partly of his own unit.

So far I have only dealt in this battle with the part of the regiment who composed the Dismounted Company at the commencement of the German offensive. I will now hark back to the 25th March. It will be remembered that it was early on the morning of this day that the 4th and 5th Dismounted Brigades rejoined their horses and "Cook's Detachment" was formed. On the same day a further effort was made to improvise some mounted troops. From the party who had been left with the led horses of the 5th Brigade, who were at Bailly, 100 men per regiment were taken to form one regiment under Colonel Fane (12th Lancers). Similar regiments were formed from the 3rd and 4th Brigades. The whole made one cavalry brigade, which was placed under the orders of Brigadier-General Pitman (the G.O.C. 4th Cavalry Brigade). This brigade marched north-east to Pontoise. The party contributed by the 20th was under the command of Lieut. Bland, but at Pontoise, Captain Hall joined and took command. This officer had been on leave, but had hastily rejoined. Fearing he would not find his revolver, which was on "B" Echelon, he had bought one in Amiens on his way through. The only one he could get was of a Spanish make. However, he armed himself with this and rushed into the fray. At 7 p.m. Colonel Fane's Regiment marched to Chiry, where they arrived at 8 p.m. Orders were then received to seize and hold Mt. Renault. This was done, but the hill was found to be already held by the French. Patrols were immediately sent to Labroye and Noyon. Both these places were reported clear of Germans. A defensive position was then taken up astride the main Noyon-Compiegne road, "C" Squadron holding Labroye brickworks.

Early on the 26th the French were compelled to evacuate Noyon, which was then occupied in strength by the enemy. Captain Hall sent the "C" Squadron Detachment under Lieut. Bland to occupy Hill 160 north-west of Labroye. About 9 a.m. it was reported that the enemy were advancing in large numbers along the Noyon-Labroye road. At 10 a.m. an order was received from Colonel Fane to concentrate at

Chapter VIII.

Passel (which is south of Labroye) as quickly as possible, as General Pitman's whole brigade was required to meet a fresh threat from some other direction. The enemy had by now penetrated between Captain Hall and " C " Squadron. A message was, however, sent to the latter by signal, and Lieut. Bland was successful in withdrawing his men without much difficulty. The Germans very soon occupied Hill 160. The ground held by the regiment was meanwhile taken over by French troops.

Colonel Fane marched to Dive-Le-Frome, where he joined General Pitman. At 2 p.m. the regiment was ordered to seize and hold Hill 104 with one squadron. This proved impracticable as the enemy were found to be already holding the hill strongly. The rest of the regiment re-inforced the 1st Squadron and a line was taken up just short of the hill. This operation was carried out with very few casualties. The horses were sent back to Ville, and at 11 p.m. the regiment was ordered to join them there. From Ville they marched to Chiry Station, where they arrived at 3 a.m. on the 27th. At noon they rejoined the 5th Cavalry Brigade near Venette, and so the brigade was enabled to re-form as a cavalry unit for the subsequent operations. The 2nd Cavalry Division was now to leave the 3rd Corps Area, and received messages from the G.O.C. 3rd Corps and from the French Commander with whom they had been working, thanking them in most complimentary terms for the work they had done.

Colonel Little had assumed command of the 20th. There were a certain number of surplus horses, owing to men having become casualties; these were left with " B " Echelon when the fighting troops moved on the 28th. On the morning of this day it was reported that the Germans had broken through south of Montdidier. The whole 2nd Cavalry Division accordingly moved via Blincourt to Noroy. Here it was learnt that the situation had been restored and that the Division would not be required. About noon a report came in that the enemy had broken through west of Montdidier and that they were advancing on the main Paris railway line at Chepoix. A prompt advance was made towards this fresh danger point, the line of march lying through Angivillers and Plainval. Once more it turned out to be a false alarm, and the division went into billets for the night about La Herrelles, which was a deserted village. The 5th Brigade formed the mounted reserve of the division and had small posts out at night, Colonel Fane being O.C. Outposts. The 3rd and 4th Brigades formed dismounted battalions in case they should be required.

On the 29th patrols were sent out at dawn to effect a liaison with the French 56th Division, who were holding the front line. The latter reported the situation as being well in hand, and at 2 p.m. the 5th Brigade marched northwards, finally going into billets at Cagny and La Boutillerie, just outside Amiens. The regiment went to the latter and got in about 8.15 p.m.

On the 30th the march was continued to the Bois L'Abbé. This was reached about 10 a.m., and about that time the weather, which had been very good for the Boche offensive so far, changed, and rain came on. The regiment remained in the wood all day and during the night. The Greys were sent to support our infantry west of the Bois de Hangard. The 12th were detailed to help the 9th Australian Brigade in a counter attack towards Aubercourt. In this affair the 12th covered themselves with glory and earned the very highest praise from even such tremendous fighters as the Australians.

The 20th remained in the wood on the 31st and organised a dismounted company of 138 all ranks under Captain Hall. In the evening a warning order was received that the 5th Dismounted Battalion would counter attack the wood known as " Rifle Wood," one mile west of Domart-Sur-Luce, early the following morning. The troops taking part in this attack were :—4th Dismounted Battalion (less Carabiniers, who were in the line), 5th Dismounted Battalion, Canadian Dismounted Battalion, 2nd Field Squadron R.E. The whole was under the command of Brigadier-General Seely, Commanding Canadian Cavalry Brigade. The 20th were to take part in the attack on the left wing. The objective was a ridge sloping up from the Luce stream, which obstacle had to be crossed first. On the ridge was the wood, the objective for the left wing of the attack including the left of the wood and some open ground outside it. The scheme for this left wing was as follows :—
1st wave, 4th Dismounted Battalion (less Carabiniers); 2nd wave, 20th Hussars. This wave was to come up on the right

of the 1st. 3rd wave, Canadian Dismounted Battalion, who were to pass through the 1st and 2nd waves. The crossing of the stream was a slow business, as it had to be done in single file along a wire fence. Fortunately this was in dead ground and not under fire. A bit short of the front edge of the wood there was a sunken lane, which it was thought would make a jumping off place for the assault of the wood. The officers of the regiment who took part in this attack were:—Captain Hall, Lieut. Taylor, Lieut. Austin, Lieut. Fairbrother. A rapid advance was made until the sunken lane was reached, and in fact the regiment was here almost in line with the first wave, though they had suffered heavy casualties. This lane was exposed to enfilade fire from guns and machine guns, which caused many casualties, including Lieuts. Taylor, Austin and Fairbrother, who were all wounded. Of the officers Captain Hall alone remained untouched. He collected the three squadrons and rushed his objective in the wood. There was hand to hand fighting here, and the Spanish revolver bought in Amiens accounted for more than one of the enemy. The Canadians passed through to the final objective while the 20th consolidated theirs. One platoon of the regiment accompanied the 3rd wave to the far edge of the wood and helped to clear it. Later a second platoon was sent up to re-inforce the Canadians. The position was held until 11.30 p.m., when the cavalry were relieved by infantry. Out of the 138 all ranks who took part in the attack, the regiment lost:—3 other ranks killed, 3 officers and 39 other ranks wounded, and one man missing.

The Greys and 12th on the right of the attack were equally successful in reaching their objective.

The following message was received from General Rawlinson, commanding 4th Army:—"I am anxious to express to the 2nd Cavalry Division my admiration and warmest thanks for their successful counter attack this morning, and I congratulate all ranks most heartily on their brilliant achievement. I fear they have suffered heavily, but their victory has been invaluable at this critical juncture."

On the 2nd April the 5th Cavalry Brigade was withdrawn to Bois L'Abbé. The strength of the regiment had been reduced to 13 officers and 150 other ranks. There were

245 horses. In the evening they were moved back further, to Camon, just east of Amiens. Here they remained till the 6th, when they were withdrawn to Buigny L'Abbé to refit. On this day our Brigade Commander, Brigadier-General C. L. K. Campbell, died in England. On the 8th Brigadier-General N. W. Haigh, of the Inniskillings, took over the Brigade. Between the 6th and 9th large re-inforcements of men, very largely from Yeomanry regiments, joined; also 2nd Lieuts. Potts and Page.

On the 9th the Germans began a fresh offensive, this time making their onslaught on the Portuguese, who were holding the line near Neuve Chapelle, in our 1st Army Area. The enemy made short work of the Portuguese and were quick to exploit the success. Our troops on either flank had to fall back, and a situation, critical for the Allies, was once more created. On the 10th the regiment was moved to Vitz Villeroy, which is on the Authie, north-west of Auxi, and 268 surplus men were sent to Long, on the Somme, for though re-inforcements in men had come up very few remounts had been received.

On the 11th the Brigade was at two hours' notice to move, as the 2nd Cavalry Division were G.H.Q. Reserve and were ready to move to the 1st Army Area. On the 12th the move started, and the regiment marched via Hesdin to Hezecque, where they arrived at 9 p.m. On the 13th they advanced to La Belle Hotesse, just east of the Aire Canal. We had last been there in October, 1914, when we moved north from the Aisne, also to meet and check a German invasion of Flanders. La Belle Hotesse, which is only a hamlet, was crowded with refugees, for the Boche in his advance had reached country that had been untouched by war since 1914. The front line now ran west of Vieux Berquin, where we had been billeted in perfect peace in 1915 and 1916.

The " Patron " from what had been a " B " Squadron farm was among the refugees at La Belle Hotesse, and the former " C " Squadron billet (Mme. Asseman's) had been burned down, destroyed by British guns.

The task now allotted to our division was to protect the left of the 1st Army about the Fôret De Nieppe, and if a gap should occur to fill it. On the 14th the regiment moved for-

Chapter VIII.

ward to the Bois Des Huit Rues and sent out liaison patrols to find out the situation. All was quiet and we returned to billets in the evening. We remained in this area until the 28th April, being continually prepared to turn out at short notice, but never being actually required. A few more re-inforcements joined, including Captain Darling, who took over "C" Squadron from Lieut. Bland; also a few horses. On the 29th, as the situation had settled down, we were withdrawn to Hezecque. Our strength on the 29th April was 19 officers and 442 other ranks.

On the 5th of May we were moved still further back to Aix-en-Issart, just east of Montreuil. Here we were very comfortable and were able to refit and generally shake down. We had got a large proportion of new officers and men and a lot of remounts. There was therefore plenty of work to do in re-organising and training. We remained in these billets until the 4th of August, except for a week in July, when we moved up to Grand Rullecourt, which is between Frevent and Arras, in support of the 3rd Army. We did not, however, become engaged. During the summer Major Mangles rejoined from the Near East and took over "B" Squadron, Major Sanford becoming 2nd in command to the regiment. The summer of 1918 was spent very pleasantly, being particularly notable for the epidemic of "flu" that swept through the whole Allied Army and, I believe, the Germans as well. In addition to training, considerable attention was paid to recreation. Under General Haigh's patronage and, indeed, active support, a very good polo ground was secured by the brigade, and the officers got a good deal of polo. In the regiment Colonel Little organised a most successful inter-troop boxing contest for teams of, I think, eight men per troop. Practically every man had to have a fight, at any rate before being eliminated from his troop team, and in this way everyone became a fighter instead of merely an onlooker, as is the case with most boxing contests. Captain Bill Adams' hefty transport drivers were soon made hot favourites; indeed it was said by many that they ought not to be allowed to compete as a troop. However, the seat of a G.S. waggon is not the best of places on which to train for a fight, and the transport were knocked out by a light but very sporting team from a troop of "A" Squadron.

In the final these in turn were rather unexpectedly beaten by the 3rd Troop of " C " (Lieut. Davy's), who had been coached by that fine old fighter, Bill Tanser, though he himself was not allowed to take part. There was also an inter-squadron officers' " contest," for teams of four. This produced some most bloodthirsty battles, and was won by " B " Squadron. Each squadron held sports, including military, athletic, and comic events, a most popular incident in which was the greasy pig contest, when our exceedingly popular C.O., Colonel Little, himself took the porker in his arms and presented it to the winners.

By August the regiment was once more in fine fighting trim and was quite ready to take its part in the great events that were destined to take place during the next two memorable months.

CHAPTER IX—August, 1918, Battle of Amiens.

(See Maps I & III).

ON the 3rd of August a Tank Corps unit held a race meeting somewhere within reach of our billets. The regiment had quite a successful day, as Lieut. Colin Davy, who was stable jockey to the regimental headquarters stud when the C.O. was unable to do the weight, won a mile flat race on " Any Time," and was just beaten in another race on " The Scone." On returning to billets in the evening the party who had been to the races were greeted by the Adjutant with the news that a " secret " message had just been received to the effect that the 5th Cavalry Brigade would march on the following evening. It is remarkable that on this occasion the news had only been received a few hours earlier by the Quartermaster, who had got it from the Mechanical Transport drivers of the Divisional Train. These men were usually in full possession of such news two or three days in advance; they were nearly always right, and they invariably spread what they had heard far and wide.

We had been at Aix so long that we had, as usual, got thoroughly settled. The 24 hours we had in which to mobilise ourselves were consequently fully occupied. Waggons had to be packed with the necessary implements of war, whilst the accessories of peace, such as polo sticks, gramophones, and mess crockery, had to be dumped somewhere in the village. While squadron-leaders and others were engaged in arranging these matters, or in making out their " states " or settling such minor affairs as " mounting up " or what horses were fit to march, they were liable at any moment to be confronted with the really serious problems of war, in the shape of bills or claims from excited civilians. These were usually presented with voluble explanations by toothless old men and women,

Lieut.-Colonel A. C. Little, D.S.O.

who talked and gesticulated at such a rate as to be quite incomprehensible. The assistance of an interpreter was then sought. The establishment of these worthies had now been reduced to two per regiment; one of these was always monopolised by Headquarters, and the other one, provided he was not " en permission," had to divide himself into three portions so as to be at the service of the three squadrons simultaneously. It would be at such a moment that a message would be received that Squadron Quartermaster-Sergeants were immediately to proceed to the Quartermaster's stores to draw equipment. We well knew what this meant. For weeks the worthy Bill Adams had been collecting such things as bayonets, picketing pegs, dixies, shackles and pack saddlery. To our entreaties that such things should be issued to us, he had in the piping times of peace turned a deaf ear. Now the order had come to move. He suddenly found he had got more stuff than he could carry. Consequently he unloaded it on to the squadrons. It must not be thought that I am crabbing the worthy Bill. No regiment ever had a better Quartermaster or one who enjoyed the more complete confidence of all ranks. The next round of the game would be for the S.Q.M.S. to load his waggon. Now the S.Q.M.S. is by nature a collector; he collects anything and everything from a complete Hotchkiss pack down to a broken baggage strap. These he hoards in the hope that they will some day come in handy. He has no idea that there is any limit to the weight that four G.S. waggon horses can draw. So it is that the Squadron Leader or his 2nd in command has to " comb out " the load on the waggon. With sorrow in his heart the S.Q.M.S. has to consign some of his museum to the regimental dump or, worse still, the salvage dump. Next the men, who while in billets have also been collecting, proceed to pack their saddles. What cannot be carried in their pockets goes in a water bucket slung over the sword hilt. Now it is the Troop Leader's turn. He proceeds to empty the water buckets. I have given this description in the hope of conveying to my civilian readers, if there were any civilians in 1918, a glimpse of the real horrors of war. These existed not on the shrapnel-swept battlefields, not in the water-logged trench, not in the mud of Flanders, nor in the shell holes of the Somme, but in their greatest intensity during the strenuous hours when we were endeavouring to break

Chapter IX.

away from peace billets and fit ourselves once more for war.

At 9 p.m. on the 4th August the regiment was on parade, thirsting for battle and pretty mobile considering that the average load of a horse was 20 stone. We moved by night, so as to elude the observation of any Boche airmen who might venture behind our lines. The blow that was to be struck by General Foch, the Allied Generalissimo, was to be unexpected by the Huns, and so it proved to be. The following officers accompanied the regiment :—

Headquarters :
Lieut.-Col. A. C. Little, in command.
Major G. A. Sanford, 2nd in command.
Captain J. H. Goodhart, Adjutant.
Lieut. G. Glover, Signalling Officer.
Lieut. L. Jones, Intelligence Officer.
Lieut. R. J. Read, Hotchkiss Gun Officer.

The latter had as his chief duty the protection of the regiment from any attack from the air. By the end of the battle he was suffering acutely from a stiff neck, from being continually on the look out for German aeroplanes.

" A " Squadron.	" B " Squadron.	" C " Squadron.
Capt. W. D. A. Hall.	Major C. G. Mangles.	Capt. J. C. Darling.
Lieut. Dodgson.	Lieut. P. S. Woolf.	Lieut. J. Cooper-Bland.
Lieut. Wyborn.	Lieut. Mitchell.	Lieut. Burt.
Lieut. F. K. Davy.	Lieut. Ralli.	Lieut. C. K. Davy.
Lieut. Jackson.	Lieut. Thorley.	Lieut. Potts.
Lieut. Brownrigg.	Lieut. Bain.	Lieut. Gunning.
Lieut. Page.	Lieut. Dawnay.	Lieut. C. Mann.

At about 2 a.m. on the 5th August we arrived at Raye-sur-Anthie. The men were in barns, the horses hidden as far as possible under hedges and in orchards. We were by now pretty good at settling into billets, even in the dark. The only people who had anything to complain of were a troop of " C " Squadron, who had to share their particular back garden with some wasps. A horse seems in the dark to have disturbed the billet or nest allotted to the latter. These showed great resentment, and the horses resented the attentions of the wasps. In the end we had to give the enemy best and find another place for the troop.

During the night 5th—6th we marched via Le Boisle and Yvrench to Oneaux, and the following night to a bivouac west of Ailly-sur-Somme. Here our brigade was pretty well concentrated, and indeed the whole 2nd Cavalry Division were not far off. Horses and men were hidden in woods and orchards, and as little movement as possible was permitted in the open during the day of the 7th. At least one Hun aeroplane came over, but he appeared not to have spotted any of us. Any way the little treat we sprung the enemy the next day took them completely by surprise.

The offensive which was to start on the 8th August was to be delivered by the French 1st Army on the right and the British 4th Army on the left. The attack was to be launched from the part of the line immediately east of Amiens, the objective being the old " Amiens Defence Line " where it had stood in 1916. The British troops to whom the attack was entrusted were, on the right, the Canadian Corps, on the left the Australian Corps. The Cavalry Corps were to exploit any success that might be achieved, the 1st Cavalry Division working with the Australians, the 2nd and 3rd with the Canadians. Zero hour was to be at 4.30 a.m. By this time the 5th Cavalry Brigade were to be at Glisy, the rest of the Cavalry Corps being in the same neighbourhood. It will thus be seen that in order to reach their position of assembly the cavalry had to pass through the " bottle neck " of Amiens.

At 11 p.m. on the 7th we started on our march through the town. Since the German advance in the spring of 1918 it was well within range of the enemy's guns, and had indeed been considerably damaged. The population had left. There was a good deal of congestion in the streets, caused by the lines of march of different units crossing one another, and at one time we were halted for an hour in the town. Fortunately the Boche had no idea of what was happening and remained very quiet. If he had started shelling Amiens he would probably have caused considerable casualties, although we kept about a hundred yards distance between squadrons and something even between troops, so as to lessen the danger. It was getting light, on a misty morning, before we were really clear of the town. We were in our appointed place at Glisy by 4.30. Here we off saddled and had breakfast, also watering and feeding the horses, as we were to be the last division of the Cavalry Corps to move. One shell fell rather uncomfortably near the brigade. It was, however, the only one and

Chapter IX.

did no damage. At 6.30 a.m. we saddled up and moved forward to a small wood one mile south of Glisy. Just before 9 a.m. we advanced along the cavalry track to the western edge of Cachy. Reports seemed to indicate that the attack was going very well, yet the curious thing about it was that everything was so silent. From where we were there was very little to indicate that a battle was in progress a few miles away. The fact was the Huns had been taken completely by surprise and were on the run.

During the morning it became known that the attack by the infantry and some whippet tanks had been a great success and that both the 1st and 3rd Cavalry Divisions had passed through the infantry and taken up the pursuit. Later reports seemed to show that the 1st Cavalry Division, advancing over the open plain that stretches away to the east of Villers Brettonneaux, were carrying all before them and meeting with very little opposition. The 5th Dragoon Guards were reported to have captured a leave train full of Germans. The 3rd Cavalry Division had, as arranged, turned south over the Luce and were engaged in the difficult wooded country that exists beyond that stream. One Cavalry Brigade was reported to be making a regular dismounted attack. In short this ground was not so favourable for mounted troops as that further north, and the cavalry were more or less held up.

At 11.45 a.m. we advanced in an easterly direction, leaving the Bois De Hangard on our right. The 2nd Cavalry Division was all pretty well concentrated, the Divisional Commander, General Pitman, was on the spot, and the G.O.C. Cavalry Corps, General Kavanagh, was also there. We were therefore momentarily expecting to be sent off to the east to still further exploit the success of the 1st Cavalry Division, and we quite began to picture ourselves then wheeling to the right and coming down on the flank or rear of the enemy who were opposing the 3rd Cavalry Division. It seemed to be the chance of a lifetime for the application of the principle of supporting the troops who were meeting with success rather than those that were held up. It seems, however, that it had previously been decided that we were to be employed on the right flank, and that therefore we had to be sent there. This arrangement seemed the more curious in view of the fact that the ground on the right was, as already mentioned, less suitable for cavalry than the ground on the left.

I have, I fear, digressed from my narrative for this criticism, which may well be quite wrong, but I do so in order to account for the feeling of disappointment which many of us experienced when we found ourselves turning south to cross the Luce at Ignaucourt in support of the 3rd Cavalry Division. On all sides were signs of the great success that had been achieved. We passed numbers of dead Germans, and there were also guns, vehicles, and other material that had been abandoned by the enemy. Everyone felt that this was indeed a great day, and that the attack was the most completely successful one that had as yet been made by the British Army. We did not realise then what we know now, that August the 8th was the beginning of the end of the German Empire as a great military machine. General Ludendorff in his book describes it as the blackest day of the whole war for the German Army.

At 1.45 p.m. we halted half a mile south of Ignaucourt. We then heard that although the 3rd Cavalry Division could not get on very much yet they could hold what they had gained, and were in no great need of support. They were fighting magnificently, as was only to be expected from such fine troops under such a determined leader as General Harman. And so it came to pass that we remained idle all the afternoon and finally at 9 p.m. pegged down for the night where we were.

For the 9th August orders were received that both the 1st and 3rd Cavalry Divisions were to be withdrawn, and that the 2nd Cavalry Division was to co-operate with the Canadian Corps between the Amiens—Roye road and the line Vrely—Fouquescourt—Hattencourt. The 5th Cavalry Brigade were detailed to operate on the right, the 3rd Cavalry Brigade on the left. I think the 4th Brigade was kept in reserve. At 9.30 a.m. the 5th Cavalry Brigade advanced to the north side of a wood to the east of Beaucourt.

Patrols were sent out from here to get in touch with the infantry and to find out the exact situation. Lieut. Potts came back and reported that the Canadian Infantry were in touch with the enemy between Le Quesnel and Beaufort. A report then came from higher authority that Beaufort was in our

Chapter IX.

hands. On receipt of this news, which I must say we did not believe in view of Lieut. Potts' very clear report, the Brigade was launched. The 20th were on the left, with Beaufort as the first objective, the Greys on the right with an objective which, I think, included Le Quesnel. " C " Squadron were the leading squadron of the regiment, and were given as the first bound a point north-east of Le Quesnel. Here the C.O. joined the Squadron Leader, while the advanced troop (the 1st Troop under Lieut. Mann) were four hundred yards further on behind a small covert. The ground just here was very flat, and it was observed that Lieut. Mann was under fire from somewhere. A Tank Corps officer reported that the whole ground in front was swept more or less by Boche machine guns. In view of this Col. Little decided not to advance direct on Beaufort, but to deviate a bit to the left into a deep gully that seemed to afford good cover. " C " Squadron were accordingly directed into this gully. The 1st Troop had some three hundred yards of very open ground to cross in order to get there, and as soon as they appeared in the open they came under heavy machine gun fire. To make matters worse there were wire fences in the way, and to get round these the troop had to pass within about five hundred yards of the Boche. It was a stirring sight to see this troop, all mounted as they were on well-bred bright chestnut horses, galloping over the plain, with the dust being kicked up all round them by the hail of bullets through which they had to pass. It was also a heart-rending scene to see many of the best of these horses, on which Charles Mann, Sergeant Phillips, and their men had lavished such infinite pains, stretched in the dust. It is remarkable that although they lost heavily in horses, I think I am right in saying not a single man was hit. On reaching the gully the troop was greeted by the Canadians, an officer of theirs being heard to remark : " That was a great gallop ; I call that sport, not war." The Hotchkiss pack pony, " Tubby," who had been a great favourite, fell dead just as the troop got under cover, and the Hotchkiss section at once came into action against the German machine guns, though it was difficult to locate these accurately. The C.O. ordered the rest of the squadron to get into the gully at a point further from the enemy. This was done, and though the three troops came under fire they were under cover before the Boche had really found the range, and only had one horse hit. Just as the squadron reached the gully the enemy started bombarding it with some " Jack Johnsons." One shell fell in the rear of the 3rd Troop (Lieut. Gunning's, since Lieut. Davy was away as a galloper) and killed three or four horses. The gully was full of tanks and Canadian Infantry, and, far from Beaufort having been taken, these troops were just lining up to attack it. Lieut. Mann joined the squadron and reported that the Huns could command the head of the gully, which ran towards them, and that it was not possible to debouch from it at that point.

This state of affairs was reported to the C.O., who eventually ordered the squadron to rejoin the regiment near Le Quesnel. The situation was not ripe for a cavalry advance, and " C " Squadron were really in the 3rd Cavalry Brigade area; in fact they had got in touch with a patrol of, I think, the 5th Lancers. The only casualty suffered by the squadron in personnel during their very uncomfortable stay in the gully was the Squadron Leader, who got a mild taste of gas and a good shaking from a shell that fell uncomfortably near him. He retired from the battle and the following day went home on a month's leave, in order to keep a matrimonial appointment. Lieut. Cooper-Bland took over the squadron.

The regiment did not move on for some hours; then at 3.30 p.m. they followed the infantry into Beaufort. From here they were unable to get on, though an attempt was made by " C " Squadron, and their 2nd Troop, under Lieut. Burt, made a most gallant reconnaissance, but drew upon themselves such heavy fire that it was soon apparent that no advance was possible. Four whippet tanks were detailed to work with the 20th, but these never turned up. If they had arrived they would probably have been invaluable and would most likely have enabled a further advance to be made, as the attack was held up chiefly by machine gun nests.

At 5.30 p.m. " A " and " C " Squadrons pushed on to the line of the Buchoir—Rouvroy road, but no further advance was possible. At 6 p.m. Headquarters and " B " Squadron moved up to the northern edge of Folies, where they spent the night close behind a weak infantry outpost line. Three posts were left out all night, one troop half a mile south

Chapter IX.

west of Warvillers, one machine gun post on the Folies—Warvillers road, and one Hotchkiss rifle post at the eastern edge of Folies.

At 7 a.m. on the 10th August the regiment was relieved by the 3rd Dragoon Guards (3rd Cavalry Division), and the 5th Brigade concentrated in a wood just south-east of Cayeux. About 3 p.m. the brigade moved up to the north-western edge of Warvillers, and at about 8 p.m. the regiment pegged down for the night at the northern edge of Beaufort. There was a lot of gas still about here, which made the men sneeze a good bit and prevented the horses grazing. Late in the afternoon of the 11th of August the regiment was withdrawn to Ignaucourt. Here they were bombed during the night from German aeroplanes, but no damage was done. No further advance was made during the 12th, 13th and 14th, and the regiment remained where they were. The German line that had been so successfully broken on the 8th of August seemed to have crystallised again, but there is no doubt that the enemy's moral had been badly shaken in this battle, and that after this he never fought quite so well again. He had now got back to the edge of the Somme battlefield. Here the ground was a wilderness of old trenches and shell holes after the successive battles that had raged over it. It was not good ground over which to carry out an energetic pursuit, and at the same time it was ideal ground for the enemy for fighting a rearguard action. Certainly it was no place for cavalry to be employed mounted, so on the 15th August the Cavalry Corps was withdrawn altogether.

The regiment marched at 9 a.m. that day via Boves and Amiens to St. Sauveur. On the 16th they did a night march, starting at 9 p.m., marching via Vignacourt, and arriving at Fieffes at 12.15 a.m. on the 17th. The following night the march was continued at 8.30 p.m., and, proceeding via Auxi Le Chateau, they arrived at Labroye at 2 a.m. on the 18th.

The regiment was now split up and employed during the rest of August as divisional cavalry. Late in the evening of the 19th August " A " and " B " Squadrons left the regiment, the former marching to Grouches, the latter to Amplier. Here they came under the 6th and 4th Corps respectively.

On the 20th " A " Squadron moved to Humbercamp

Lieuts. F. K. Davy and Brownrigg going off in charge of detachments for duty with the 3rd Division and a Battalion of the Tank Corps respectively. Here they were employed finding liaison patrols and despatch riders during active operations. They suffered a few casualties in men and horses. On the 23rd an attack was made by our infantry and tanks on Bihucourt, Sapignies and Behagnies. Parties from the squadron under Lieuts. Page and Davy took part in this attack. Meanwhile Lieut. Brownrigg's troop was with the 2nd Division at Gomiecourt, and Lieut. Dodgson had a troop at Ransart working under the Guards Division. The different parties were relieved from Squadron Headquarters at intervals, and on the 30th the squadron was collected once more at Humbercamp. During the evening of this day they rejoined Regimental Headquarters at Warlincourt, to which place the latter had moved on the 21st.

"B" Squadron reached Amplier at 3 a.m. on the 20th, and the following night sent three troops off on detachment. At 4 a.m. on the 21st the 3rd Troop arrived at Fouquevillers and were sent on to an advanced position for duty with the 15th Infantry Brigade. The 1st Troop remained at Fouquevillers for liaison duty with the 5th Division. The 4th Troop reached Souastre about 5 a.m. on the 21st after marching all night, and were sent on to reconnoitre the line Ablainzeville—Achiet-le-Grand. The 2nd Troop also left Amplier early on the 21st and marched to Souastre, where they joined the 63rd Division. From the 22nd to the 25th most of the squadron were employed on liaison duties, sustaining a certain number of casualties. On the 25th Squadron Headquarters were established at Achiet-le-Grand and liaison work continued till the 30th, when the squadron was collected. They rejoined Regimental Headquarters on the 31st.

"C" Squadron left the regiment, or what remained of it, on the 20th, the 1st and 4th Troops (Lieuts. Mann and Potts) going to Doullens, where they reported to the Provost Marshal 3rd Army. The 2nd Troop (Lieut. Burt) went to Coigneux, and the 3rd Troop (Lieut. C. K. Davy) to Humbercamp. All were employed chiefly escorting prisoners of war. On the 24th August the squadron was sent to the 5th Corps as Corps Cavalry. The 1st and 4th Troops (under Lieut. Bland) were

Chapter IX.

attached to the 38th Division, the 2nd to the 21st Division, the 3rd to the 17th Division. Lieut. Bland's party were lucky in meeting old friends of the regiment. The 38th Division was commanded by Major-General Tom Cubitt, whom we had known well from 1908 to 1910 as Brigade Major 3rd Cavalry Brigade in Ireland. In addition to this his A.A. and Q.M.G. was Colonel Romer Lee, who had been Adjutant to the 20th during the South African War, and who had later commanded first the Reserve Squadron and then " A " Squadron. He may also be said to have been the founder of the Regimental Polo Club, and he led the team to victory in their first inter-regimental triumph in India. He also later assisted them to win the home inter-regimental in 1907. Both the General and Colonel Lee received this detachment of the regiment with the greatest hospitality. As was only natural, General Cubitt knew well how to make use of cavalry in action. His division were attacking on the 26th and 27th, and good work was done by the half-squadron in assisting the advance and in keeping touch with the divisions on the flanks.

During the 27th patrols from the squadron, one of them led by S.S.M. Adams, were sent on in advance of the infantry to keep touch with the retreating enemy. The 2nd Troop was also usefully employed on advanced guard work by the 21st Division. On the 29th the 3rd Troop got a show, being attached to the 115th Infantry Brigade and used to regain touch with the Germans, who had retired during the previous night in the neighbourhood of Morval and Les Boeufs. On the 31st the squadron was collected and rejoined the regiment at Warlincourt.

CHAPTER X—The Last Push.

(See Map III).

THE regiment remained at Warlincourt until the 6th of September, on which day the whole 5th Cavalry Brigade was concentrated just south of Albert, being attached to the 4th Army and held ready to exploit the success of an attack that was to be made by the Australian Corps. This was not made, however, and the regiment moved back to Behencourt. They remained here till the 26th September, doing training for open warfare. While they were here the following officers rejoined from the United Kingdom:—Captain Darling, Lieuts. Taylor, Groves, Read, Jackson. Lieut. Woodman was seconded for duty with the Signal Service.

At 7.30 p.m. on the 26th we started from Behencourt to take part in the last great offensive of the war, though in reality a steady pressure had been kept on the Huns ever since the memorable 8th of August. We marched via Hamelet and at midnight arrived at Cerizy, near Prozart. Here we were accommodated in the ruins of the village. During the night 27th—28th we continued the march via Brie to Le Mesnil Bruntel, where we spent the remainder of the night in tin huts erected by the British before the Boche offensive in March, 1918, and that had somehow survived successive attempts by both sides at their destruction. We stayed here all the 28th, and moved on at 8 a.m. on the 29th, to take part in the battle. On this day an American Corps and the Australian Corps were attacking the Hindenburg Line beyond Roisel. We were to pass through the 5th Australian Division when they reached what was known as the " Beaurevoir Line." We marched via Cartigny and Hamel to Roisel, where we watered the horses. At 12.45 p.m. we reached Templeux Le Guerrard, and at

Chapter X.

1.30 p.m. we arrived at our jumping off place in a valley west of Hargicourt. Here everything was in readiness for the pursuit. The regiment was in Brigade Reserve, but "A" and "B" Squadrons were told off, in the event of a break through, to destroy the railway at Bohain and Busigny. The O.C. "B" Squadron and his versatile 2nd in command spent their spare moments in making up a little ditty on the "— Busigny Railway." I don't remember it very well, and perhaps there are also other reasons why it had better not appear in print. We soon discovered that part of the infantry attack was held up, and as the afternoon wore on it became evident that we should not be employed that day. The ground where we were had been heavily shelled before our arrival, and I regret to say that one troop of "C" Squadron (the 4th) suffered severely from gas poisoning as a result of drinking tea made with water from a shell hole. It is unfortunate that some of the tea was drunk by the Sergeants' Mess. By night every member of the mess had gone sick except S.S.M. Adams. That most gallant warrant officer was himself poisoned and was suffering agonies, but he refused to give in and stuck it out somehow. As a result of this the squadron was very weak afterwards, especially in N.C.O.'s. One Sergeant, I think Sergeant Brook, was at duty afterwards, as I fancy he was on leave at the time. The 2nd Troop were also all right, as they had been detached the day before for duty with the 46th Division. At 7.15 p.m. we moved back to a bivouac just outside Roisel. It was a pouring wet night and there was great congestion on the road.

On the 30th the regiment moved off at 11.30 a.m. and marched viâ Hervilly and Jeancourt to a valley north-west of Verguier. The brigade was now under the orders of the 9th Corps. What was left of "C" Squadron, consisting of two officers and about forty men, were sent off for duty with the 32nd Division. The Hindenburg Line had now been captured, as had the line of the Canal De St. Quentin. Our infantry were in touch with the enemy east of the canal, the line in the part of the front that concerned us running roughly through Nauroy and Magny La Fosse.

"C" Squadron reported to the 32nd Division at their advanced headquarters, which was in the old Hindenburg Line on the high ground north-west of Bellenglise. The Divisional Commander (Major-General Lambert) explained to the Squadron Leader that he intended to attack the following afternoon, and that he wanted the squadron to push on after the attack and keep in touch with the enemy.

At 8 a.m. on the 1st of October, Colonel Little and the O.C. " C " Squadron attended a conference held in an old German dug-out just east of Bellenglise, at which this attack was discussed in detail. The salient features of this conference were as follows :—(1) The Huns were supposed to be in the last ditch, that is to say, they were said to be holding a trench line running just south of Joncourt, and from there about through Levergies. Beyond this line there were no more trenches. (2) The 32nd Division had already done a lot of fighting, and had suffered heavy losses. Their numbers were weak, and the men were tired. All three brigades were in the front line : there was no divisional reserve. (3) They were, however, determined to attack and take this last trench line. (4) The brigade that seemed to be in the best fighting trim was the one that was to attack opposite Joncourt. " C " Squadron was attached to this brigade, and it was arranged that as soon as they had taken the objective they should fill in a bit of trench and clear the wire at a point just south of Joncourt. The squadron would then pass through and get in touch with the enemy. It was decided that this could, however, not happen until a German strong point known as " Swiss Cottage " had been taken. When this and the trench line was in the hands of our infantry, a white rocket would be fired, and that would be the signal for the squadron to start.

In accordance with these arrangements, at 4 p.m. the squadron, such as it was, was assembled in a valley just north of the Bellenglise-Joncourt road. In addition to the Squadron Leader, there was only one officer present, Lieut. Mann; Lieut. Burt was detached with his troop, and the others must have been on leave. The squadron watched the artillery " creeping barrage " moving forward, and knew that behind this our infantry were advancing. The Boche retaliated by putting down a barrage of gas shells behind the infantry. This necessitated the squadron being kept a bit further back than had been intended, for, though the men had box respirators, the horses were unprotected. As time went by and no white rocket was seen, it began to be feared that the attack had failed. The Squadron Leader rode over to the Infantry Brigade Advanced Headquarters to find out, and was there informed that all the objectives had been taken and that the cavalry could advance. At the same time, he was handed a fresh lot of orders from General Neil Haigh. These required that three strong patrols should be sent to points named, all south-west of Ramicourt, and that these should remain out as standing patrols all night. After deducting the Hotchkiss sections, the provision of these patrols took every man in the squadron. The patrols were quickly detailed, under Lieut. Mann, S.S.M. Adams and Sergeant Brook. These were despatched on their missions, while the Squadron Leader took the Hotchkiss sections to Magny La Fosse, where he heard the 5th Cavalry Brigade ought to be. He intended borrowing another troop from the regiment, and with this and the Hotchkiss sections he then meant to go to the gap in the trench line, there to act as a support to the patrols. The latter had been directed to send reports to that point. On reaching Magny La Fosse, it was found that the 20th were still some way in rear; the Brigade-Major was, however, encountered, and he promised to ask the C.O. to send a troop. Meanwhile, the O.C. " C " borrowed half-a-dozen sturdy 12th Lancers from Colonel Fane, and galloped forward to the " gap." Just as he got there, he met the remnants of S.S.M. Adams' patrol coming back. This patrol had come under heavy fire as they were crossing the gap, and every man had been hit. The infantry were exhausted, and were all taking cover as best they could. There was not a rifle or machine gun going to afford covering fire—in addition to this, the slope opposite contained several hidden machine gun nests, and " Swiss Cottage," far from being in our hands, still sheltered some German machine guns that were bringing heavy fire to bear on the " gap." It was under these conditions that S.S.M. Adams had attempted to gallop his patrol across the trenches. I feel sure that no more gallant or futile effort has been made since the charge of the Light Brigade at Balaclava. The Squadron Leader was just in time to prevent Lieut. Mann's making a similar attempt, for he too meant going. The cavalry were out to justify their existence at last, and nothing but a definite order to rally behind the crest line would have stopped them. S.S.M. Adams was hit in the leg, but was intent on going forward to look for a wounded man of his whose horse had been killed. It required a very stern order before he could be induced to go to the Field Ambulance instead. Even so he rejoined the next day. As the squadron were rallying, Lieut. Jackson's troop of " A " Squadron arrived to support them, but it was useless to try and push on. The whole 5th Cavalry Brigade pegged down near Magny La Fosse for the night. Soon after midnight the Brigadier received orders from the 9th Corps to push one regiment through in the morning. General Neil Haigh pointed out that in his opinion such an operation would have no chance of success, and would merely result in the waste of lives that might be invaluable later on. The G.O.C. 9th Corps then cancelled the order. Later in the day the 12th Lancers made an attempt to advance, but suffered considerable casualties, and had to retire. The Brigade moved back to south of the Verguier for the night. They came in for a good bit of shelling, but the only casualty suffered by the regiment was one horse killed.

The 3rd of October was to be a quiet day; however, at 11.30 a.m., news was received that an attack by the 46th Division was going well. The regiment was rushed off via Magny La Fosse to Presselles, but found that the infantry were held up and that there was no opportunity for the employment of cavalry. During the afternoon a German counter-attack developed against Montbrehain. The ground where the regiment was assembled was shelled, and Lieut. Mann was killed, Lieut. Leslie Jones was wounded, and Lieut. F. K. Davy and three other ranks were badly gassed. During the time he had been with the Regiment, Charles Mann had shown himself to be a very dashing cavalry officer and a very good troop leader. He was the sort of officer we could ill afford to lose. The Regiment rejoined the remainder of the brigade east of Magny La Fosse, and in the evening a dismounted battalion, under Colonel Little, was hastily formed from the brigade on a report that the enemy had established themselves on the railway west of Presselles. This report turned out to be untrue. The infantry line in that neighbourhood was, however, very weak, so the battalion occupied a line running round the north, east and south-east of Presselles. The 12th and Greys were in the front line, and the 20th in support. After a quiet night, the battalion was relieved by some infantry during the 4th. That evening the brigade was withdrawn to Le Verguier, where they remained till the 8th. That day " A " Squadron were sent as far as the Ramicourt-Bohain railway on receipt of a report that the 3rd Cavalry Division had gone through the gap at that point. The report turned out to be quite untrue, and the squadron rejoined the brigade south-west of Magny La Fosse. On the 9th the regiment went forward to a valley south-west of Montbrehain, but returned later to Presselles. On the 10th a definite advance was made to Brancoucourt and the western edge of Bohain. At this time the regiment was ready to take part in an advance of the Cavalry Corps on Le Cateau.

On the 11th, " A " Squadron were sent forward to keep touch with the infantry of the 9th Corps between Molain and Andigny Les Fermes. No advance was possible, but Lieut. Jackson was killed while in charge of a liaison patrol, the regiment thus losing a very gallant officer.

On the 12th October, our brigade was split up, each regiment being sent to a different corps as corps cavalry. The 20th were allotted to the 2nd American Corps, and moved to a bivouac at Sablière Wood, which is just north-west of Bohain. This was a damp and uncomfortable spot, and there seemed to be no likelihood of our being immediately required for active operations. The Colonel accordingly requested the Americans to allot us a billet, but they replied that there was no billet available. Our C.O., who always had the comfort of the regiment at heart, was not to be put off so easily, so he started to look for a billet himself. He found what seemed a suitable place at Vaux Le Pretre. There were the remains of a substantial house here, to which the Huns had added a number of huts and a lot of tin stables. Unfortunately, three American battalions were quartered there. Colonel Little, however, tackled the American Corps Headquarters, and eventually " old soldiered " them into agreeing to turn out the three battalions and give us the place. Captain Sparrow, who had rejoined and was with regimental headquarters, was sent with an advanced party to take over. He found the " Allied and Associated Powers" still in possession, and quite unaware that they had got to move. He also found some men of theirs busy with picks trying to dig a hole in the stone courtyard for the purpose of burying a dead horse. He suggested to a Colonel who was present that it would be easier digging elsewhere, whereupon the following order was issued : " Say, boys, I guess you had better drag that horse outside and get busy digging a hole there." By the time the regiment arrived, and the order that the place was to be handed over had been received, the horse had been disposed of. Some of our men were heard to complain to the Yanks that they were a bit slow in turning out, but the latter " guessed " that we need not be in too great a hurry, seeing that we had been trying to take the Hindenburgh Line for three years, whereas they had done the job in fifteen minutes. In the end everything was amicably arranged, and we got settled in.

The place was rather unsavoury until we had cleaned it up and buried some more dead horses that were lying about. On the 14th the O.C. " C " Squadron went home sick, and Captain Sparrow took over the squadron.

During the 15th and 16th, troops of " C " Squadron went to near Busigny for duty with the 27th American Division. On the 17th an attack was made by the 2nd American Corps and the 9th and 13th British Corps on the line of the canal which runs through Catillon. " B " and " C " Squadrons were employed finding liaison patrols and despatch riders, headquarters and " A " Squadron moved up to just south of St. Souplet. The attack did not meet with much success, and the regiment returned to Vaux Le Pretre in the evening. " C " Squadron alone remained out, spending the night near Busigny. On the 18th the attack was resumed and the infantry made an advance of three thousand yards. There was, however, no opportunity for employing cavalry except as liaison patrols and despatch riders. During the night of the 18th-19th, the regiment was disposed : Headquarters and " A " Squadron at Vaux Le Pretre, " B " Squadron north of Molain, " C " Squadron near Busigny. On the 20th " B " and " C " Squadrons rejoined headquarters at Vaux Le Pretre. On the 21st the whole 5th Cavalry Brigade (less 12th Lancers) was reformed and attached to the 1st British Division.

Chapter X.

During the 22nd and night of 22nd-23rd, two troops from " A " Squadron were attached to the 2nd and 3rd Infantry Brigades, who were making a local attack. On the 26th two troops of " B " Squadron were sent to Busigny to work with the 6th Division (9th Corps). On the 27th the 5th Cavalry Brigade (less 12th Lancers and 20th Hussars) moved to Le Verguier. The regiment meanwhile remained at Vaux Le Pretre, where, on the 1st of November, they came under the 32nd Division. On the 3rd " B " Squadron were away finding detachments to work with infantry brigades.

On the 4th November the 32nd Division attacked the Sambre and Oise Canal. The regiment was under the orders of the 97th Infantry Brigade, which was the reserve brigade of the division. At 9.30 a.m. they marched for St. Souplet, where they arrived at noon. In the afternoon they moved on to Bazouel. " A " Squadron were detached and came under the orders of the 46th division, whom they joined at L'Arbre Du Guise. They did not rejoin until after " Cease Fire " on the 11th.

At 7.30 a.m. on the 5th November, the 97th Infantry Brigade passed through the two leading brigades (the 96th and 14th), the 20th going with them. " C " Squadron were employed during the subsequent advance, two troops and eight machine guns (attached from the 5th Machine Gun Squadron) under Captain Sparrow being lent to a battalion of the Argyle and Sutherland Highlanders, who were on the left, two troops under Lieut. Bland to the 5th Battalion Border Regiment, who were on the right. Captain Sparrow's troops were to protect the left flank of the infantry during the advance, and succeeded in doing this, advancing as far as La Basse Maroilles, where they were held up by heavy machine gun fire. They captured three prisoners. Lieut. Bland was ordered to act as advanced guard to the Border Regiment. He advanced at 7.40 a.m. and took Favril, where he captured two eight-inch guns and forty-nine prisoners. On entering the village he found that his vanguard commander, the O.C. 3rd Troop, had captured not only all the Germans in the place, but also the affections of the prettiest girl in the village. Anyway, she had her hands clasped round his neck, and was welcoming him as her deliverer. The 3rd Troop were, of course, immediately ordered on to the next bound, while rumour has it that the squadron second in command took the place vacated by his subordinate ! Lieut. Bland, however, tore himself away and pushed on another two miles before being held up by Boche machine guns. He took up a position here with his two troops, and was eventually relieved by the infantry. During the day the squadron lost two men killed, and Lieut. Denchfield and two other ranks wounded. The remainder of the regiment advanced at 9 a.m. to Rue Verte, and at noon to Favril. Here " C " Squadron rejoined them during the afternoon. Lieut. Denchfield had taken over the 1st Troop of " C " Squadron after Lieut. Mann had been killed, and had done very well.

On the 6th the regiment passed through the infantry on the line of the Maroilles-Prisches road. The enemy were found to be holding Petite Helpe. The stream in front was unfordable and all the bridges had been destroyed, except the one at Maroilles, which was outside the 97th Brigade area. At 1.35 p.m. the regiment crossed by this bridge, leaving " B " Squadron at Le Grand Fayt. A strong German outpost line was discovered north of the stream along the Taisnieres Le Grand Fayt road, and no more progress was made. The night was spent in some farms about a mile and a half east of Maroilles. In the course of this day the 25th Division (on the left of the 32nd) had reached the line of the Dompierre-Cartigny road, so during the night of the 6th-7th the 97th Brigade advanced to that line without opposition.

At 7.15 a.m. on the 7th the advance was continued, the regiment passing through the infantry and getting on to within one mile of Avesnes. Here they were held up by a line of German machine gun posts. The infantry came up at 10.30 a.m., but no further advance was made that day. The regiment, however, left patrols out in touch with the enemy. While in command of one of these, S.S.M. Adams galloped into the midst of a party of the enemy, and was wounded and taken prisoner. Other casualties suffered by the regiment were Captain Clark (the Medical Officer) and one man killed, seven other ranks wounded. The night 7th-8th was spent at Autreppes.

Orders for the 8th were that the regiment should again

pass through the infantry at 7.15 a.m. Mounted patrols were sent out earlier than this, and these reported that the Germans were still holding the same line as on the previous day. No further mounted advance was possible before noon. By that hour our infantry had established themselves in the northern edge of Avesnes, whereupon the enemy evacuated the town. Mounted patrols of " B " Squadron that had been out since dawn, under Lieuts. Michell and Ralli, at once pushed on north and south of Avesnes, and, passing round the town, met at Flaumont. The 97th Infantry Brigade advanced through Avesnes and dug in on the eastern edge of it. The " B " Squadron patrols were then withdrawn. On their way back Lieut. Ralli's patrol passed a railway truck full of ammunition that was on fire; it blew up just as they were going by, killing one man and wounding Lieut. Ralli and two other ranks, Lieut. Ralli dying in hospital on the 14th November.

In Lieut. Ralli the regiment lost a very promising young officer. He had only joined recently, and I fancy he went into action for the first time at the Battle of Amiens. His death was particularly sad, occurring, as it did, three days after the end of hostilities; in fact, on the 11th of November his relations had not even heard that he was wounded.

The 46th Division, who were on the right of the 32nd, failed to advance at first, so the regiment was employed to form a defensive flank facing south. Eventually the 46th Division came up into line, and the regiment was withdrawn to Belle Fontaine for the night.

At 7.45 a.m. on the 9th, the 20th once more passed through the infantry and advanced without opposition viâ Flaumont, the northern edge of Semeries, and Rempsies to Pont De La Ville. Here they were on the extreme eastern edge of the most eastern maps that had been issued, and were five miles in advance of the infantry. They were also unable to gain touch with any British unit on either flank. Three miles further to the east our patrols got in touch with the Germans at Touvent. The regiment spent the night at Pont De La Ville. I think I am right in saying that this was only the second occasion in the war when the 20th spent a night completely isolated from other troops. The previous occasion when this had happened was in October, 1914, at Tenbrielen.

I may mention here that during these operations Major Sanford was in command of the regiment, which consisted of Headquarters, "B" and "C" Squadrons, "A" being detached. Colonel Little was in charge of the 5th Cavalry Brigade, the Brigadier being away. During the night 9th-10th no orders were received, as all bridges west of Pont De La Ville had been destroyed, and a lot of damage had also been done to the roads. In the absence of orders, Major Sanford decided to push on on the 10th. Patrols were accordingly sent out at dawn, and these located some German machine guns in the south-west corner of the Bois De Nostriment. The regiment turned the southern flank of this position, and the enemy withdrew. A continuous line of Boche machine guns was, however, discovered running north and south along a spur north-west of Eppe Sauvage. At 10.30 a.m. an order reached the regiment that they now formed part of "Bethell's Force," a body consisting of the 5th Cavalry Brigade and two infantry brigades. This force had been formed to act as advanced guard to the 4th Army, since, owing to the damage done by the enemy to roads and railways, it was found impossible to feed a larger force. The objective of "Bethell's Force" for the 10th was to form a bridgehead beyond the Beaumont stream from Renlies inclusive, to Fourbechies exclusive.

This changed the direction of the advance from east to north-east. The regiment sent out a fresh advanced guard, who soon got in touch, just north of the Bois De Toutvent, with a continuation of the same line of machine guns that had already been discovered further south. The 12th Lancers on the left were held up by a similar lot of machine guns west of Sivry. No further advance was possible. It will be noticed that the regiment had now crossed the frontier and penetrated once more into Belgium. No British troops had previously been in quite this part of Belgium all through the war, as Binche lies fifteen or twenty miles further north. In the evening the 20th returned to sleep in France at a farm south-east of Clair Fayts. The situation of the regiment on this night seems to call for some comment. The billet was within a mile of the German line, but, as the enemy had little fight left the danger was more apparent than real. Owing to the

Chapter X.

destruction of the roads and to our forward position, it was not possible to get up rations on the nights of either November 9th or 10th. Consequently, the " iron ration " was consumed on the 10th. (No, gentle reader, an " iron ration " is not so hard and unpalatable as it sounds; it is actually a lump of bully beef contained in an iron or, more correctly, a tin covering. In simple language, it is a tin of bully beef carried by every man as an emergency ration, and only consumed in real emergencies on the order of some senior officer.) When this was consumed, the last available reserve in the food line had been thrown in: there was no hope of " living on the country "; the Boche had seen to that. As a result, there was no alternative on the morning of the 11th but to await the arrival of the ration waggons. Patrols were, however, pushed forward, for at 9.30 a.m. a message was received from the 66th Division announcing the impending armistice, and requesting that some troops should advance as far as possible, so as to be in possession of certain ground at the cessation of hostilities. Lieut. Dawnay (" B " Squadron) and Lieut. Burt (" C " Squadron) were sent forward with their troops to fulfil this mission. Lieut. Dawnay had not come into contact with the enemy by 11 a.m., when the Armistice commenced. Lieut. Burt was engaged at that hour in stalking a German machine gun near Sivry Station, and it was only on a staff officer insisting that the war was over that this very gallant and energetic officer, who, by the way, had obtained his commission from the ranks of the Leicester Yeomanry, was persuaded to desist. We can therefore claim that men of the 20th Hussars were among the last as well as the first British troops to be engaged with the Germans in the Great War.

I must now go back to the 4th November, and briefly recount the experiences of " A " Squadron. On that day, Captain Hall had orders to take his squadron and join the 46th Division. He accordingly reported to them at L'Arbre Du Guise. At 4 a.m. on the 5th November, the squadron crossed the canal at a lock south of Catillon, and at 5.30 a.m. they passed through the infantry outposts and advanced towards Prisches. Two mounted patrols were sent forward, towards Petit Be'ard and Le Sart respectively, but both were held up by machine gun fire.. The squadron was then ordered to co-operate with the 138th Infantry Brigade in the taking of Le Sart. They moved round the southern flank of the village, and the Boche cleared out. They then held the place until relieved by the infantry, returning at 4 p.m. to billets at La Groise. The squadron's casualties in this affair amounted to one man and three horses killed.

On the 6th the squadron left billets at 4 a.m., a patrol under Lieut. Dodgson passing through the 139th Infantry Brigade. This patrol reported a German outpost line a short distance east of Prisches. The squadron remained at Petit Be'ard and spent the night there. On the 7th, they moved during the afternoon to Catigny, where they came under the orders of the 137th Infantry Brigade. At 5 a.m. on the 8th, they advanced from Catigny and got in touch with the enemy, who were found to be holding a line half a mile east of the Avesnes-Etroeungt road. Here they were relieved by the infantry, who were held up there for the rest of the day. On the 9th the G.O.C. 46th Division ordered the Squadron Leader to push on and support a squadron of the Greys who were east of Sains Du Nord. Captain Hall got in touch with this squadron at 3 p.m., but the Greys reported that all the bridges were destroyed, and that they could not advance any further. "A" Squadron spent the night at Sains Du Nord.

On the 10th the squadron came under "Bethell's Force," but received no orders, so they remained where they were. By the morning of the 11th no orders had yet been received, but Captain Hall had discovered that General Bethell was at Solre Le Chateau, so he marched the squadron there and reported to the General at 9.30 a.m. He then got orders to join the 199th Brigade at Clair Fayts, and to get in touch with the enemy near Sivry. Just short of Sivry he was met by the Brigade Major, 199th Brigade, who halted the squadron, as it was now 10.50 and the war was due to end in ten minutes! "A" Squadron rejoined the regiment.

They found Major Sanford and most of "B" and "C" Squadrons still awaiting the arrival of rations. At 11 a.m. the trumpeters of the regiment were assembled outside regimental headquarters, where they sounded "Cease Fire," while everyone tried to realise that one of the greatest chapters

Chapter X.

in the world's history had closed. There was a little cheering, and everyone expressed themselves as being very glad that it was over. In a few moments, however, some of the more ardent spirits were discussing with regret what to them had been the pleasanter incidents of the war. Hardly had the " Cease Fire " sounded than the ration waggons appeared on the skyline. These were greeted with even greater enthusiasm than had been the armistice itself. During the morning, the G.O.C. 32nd Division visited the Brigadier personally, and thanked him for the good work done by the 20th during the closing scenes of the war. With the rations arrived a mail, including as good luck would have it a case of whisky for the O.C. " A " Squadron. D'Arcy Hall, with his usual hospitality, invited all the officers to dine with him that night, and though he was unfortunately taken ill at the last moment and was unable to attend, I regret to say that not a drop of that whisky remained undrunk the next morning.

The following officers were present on 11th November :—

Headquarters.

Major Sanford, D.S.O.; Captain Goodhart, M.C.; Lieut. Glover.

" A " Squadron.

Captain Hall, M.C.; Lieut. Dodgson, Lieut. Wyborn, Lieut. Page, Lieut. Brownrigg.

" B " Squadron.

Major Mangles, M.C.; Lieut. P. S. Woolf, Lieut. Thorley, Lieut. Michell, Lieut. Bain, Lieut. Dawnay.

" C " Squadron.

Captain Sparrow, M.C.; Lieut. Cooper Bland, M.C.; Lieut. C. K. Davy, M.C.; Lieut. Groves, Lieut. Burt.

If I have omitted any from this historic list, I must apologise. It is as near as I can get.

Now the rest of the acts of the 20th Hussars and all that they did—how they polished up their accoutrements and marched through Belgium, how at one place a local Bolshevik stole the kits belonging to " B " Squadron, how they occupied Burg Reuland in Germany, how they returned to Le Sart near Spa in Belgium, how Myles Thompson and others constructed the Spa steeplechase course under the patronage of the Brigadier, how Arthur Little, Jimmy Lethbridge and Colin

Davy carried off all the best trophies with Any Time, Daly Lad and Solomon, how the regiment was reduced to a " Cadre," how we none of us knew the correct pronunciation of this word, nor whether it was French or English, how the said cadre returned to Colchester, whence the regiment had set out for the war four and a half years before, how they were brought up to strength again, how in the summer of 1919 they proceeded to the Land of Egypt under Colonel M.E. Richardson, D.S.O., how they dealt with the Turkish rebels in Asia Minor, how Major Mangles hunted the hounds and dealt with the foxes and hares of Asia Minor, how the regiment was disbanded, scrapped to provide some tanks, how they rose again (as a phœnix from its own ashes) in the form of one squadron, how they now form part of the 14th/20th Hussars —are not these matters beyond the scope of this modest volume?

There only remains for me to wish this remnant of the regiment the best of luck in the future. Most of the old 20th are scattered far and wide throughout the cavalry and civilian life, and not a few are sleeping their last sleep on the battlefields of France and Belgium. All friends of the regiment, and they are many, will join with me in an expression of satisfaction that the squadron is commanded by so good a soldier as Major Mangles. Throughout his service he has done a tremendous lot for the regiment, and no officer can be found who possesses in greater measure the spirit which, in peace and in war, has always animated "Nobody's Own."

On the eve of " going to Press," news has reached me that Major Mangles is leaving the service to become M.F.H. of the H.H. Again I say good luck to him in his new capacity; and to his successor, whoever he may be, in command of the squadron.

www.ingramcontent.com/pod-product-compliance
Lightning Source LLC
Chambersburg PA
CBHW070909160426
43193CB00011B/1409